DATE DUE

DEMCO 38-296

GREAT WRITERS OF THE ENGLISH LANGUAGE

Two English Masters

TAFF CREDITS

Executive Editor
Reg Wright

Series Editor
Sue Lyon

Editors
Jude Welton
Sylvia Goulding

Deputy Editors
Alice Peebles
Theresa Donaghey

Features Editors
Geraldine McCaughrean
Emma Foa
Ian Chilvers

Art Editors
Kate Sprawson
Jonathan Alden
Helen James

Designers
Simon Wilder
Frank Landamore

Senior Picture Researchers
Julia Hanson
Vanessa Fletcher
Georgina Barker

Picture Clerk
Vanessa Cawley

Production Controllers
Judy Binning
Tom Helsby

Editorial Secretaries
Fiona Bowser
Sylvia Osborne

Managing Editor
Alan Ross

Editorial Consultant
Maggi McCormick

Publishing Manager
Robert Paulley

Reference Edition Published 1989
Published by Marshall Cavendish Corporation
147 West Merrick Road
Freeport, Long Island
N.Y. 11520

Typeset by Litho Link Ltd., Welshpool
Printed and Bound in Italy by
L.E.G.O. S.p.a. Vicenza

LIBRARY OF CONGRESS
Library of Congress Cataloging-in-Publication Data
Great Writers of the English Language
p. cm.
Includes index vol.
ISBN 1-85435-000-5 (set): $399.95
1. English literature — History and criticism. 2. English
literature — Stories, plots, etc. 3. American literature — History
and criticism. 4. American literature — Stories, plots, etc.
5. Authors. English — Biography. 6. Authors. American — Biography.
I. Marshall Cavendish Corporation.
PR85.G66 1989
820'.9 – dc19   88-21077
                                                    CIP

ISBN 1–85435–000–5 (set)
ISBN 1–85435–003–X (vol)

GREAT WRITERS OF THE ENGLISH LANGUAGE

Two English Masters

Charles Dickens

Thomas Hardy

MARSHALL CAVENDISH · NEW YORK · TORONTO · LONDON · SYDNEY

CONTENTS

CHARLES DICKENS

→ 1812-1870 ←

Charles Dickens was the greatest novelist of his time and, as well
as being a creator of memorable and colourful characters, he was
essentially a subversive writer. He made his readers think and feel
and *act* in a way that was new. Though he came to be embraced
by the Establishment of his own time, Dickens spent his life
fighting its tyranny and injustice. When he died, a cabman's
testimonial summed him up: 'Ah, Mr Dickens was a great man
and a true friend of the poor'.

Tragedy and Triumph

Dickens achieved immense literary success and public acclaim, but his private life was haunted by traumatic childhood experiences and an unsatisfied quest for emotional fulfilment.

Few writers have written so movingly about, or captured so completely the inner workings of the child's mind as Charles Dickens. Dickens never lost the feeling of what it was like to be a child or to see as a child. And the memory of childhood – 'the best and purest link between this world and a better' – is recollected and retold again and again in his novels and short stories.

Dickens' own childhood began in a tiny terraced house in Landport, near Portsmouth, on 7 February 1812, a few hours after his mother, Elizabeth, had returned from a dance. His father, John Dickens was verbose, kind-hearted, hospitable and generous. He worked as a clerk at the Navy pay office, but he was chronically incapable of living within his means.

The second of seven children, Charles – as he himself said – was 'a very little . . . very sickly boy', subject to violent 'spasms'. These spasms recurred at times of unhappiness and stress throughout his life.

A HAPPY BEGINNING

When Charles was two years old, his father was transferred to London, where the family lived in lodgings in Norfolk Street. Three years later, they settled at Chatham in Kent. Here, Charles spent some of the happiest days of his life. Later, he was to recall those far-off days with almost bitter nostalgia.

But Dickens was no sentimentalist when it came to depicting childhood. He knew from his own experience that fear – fear of the unknown and fear of being ridiculed and of not being understood – plays a large part in the life of a child. Young Charles, an unusually imaginative and sensitive boy, suffered more than most. Nightly, his nurse Mary Weller fed his fertile

A pastoral idyll
(above) In the heart of the Kent countryside that so delighted Dickens as a boy, Rochester and Chatham provide settings for both Great Expectations *and* David Copperfield. *Inclined to be nostalgic, Dickens was to comment later, 'everything wore a richer and more brilliant hue than it is ever dressed in now'. Fond memories of those days led him to buy a second home there.*

Dickens' parents
(right) John and Elizabeth, taken from contemporary engravings. Young Charles accompanied his father to inns and public houses where he sang songs and recited stories, to be tipped with meals and drink. In later life, his parents unashamedly lived on Dickens' credit, even selling scraps of his discarded manuscripts. 'It is a melancholy truth that even great men have their poor relations.'

Marshalsea Prison
(above) Dickens' family
was imprisoned here for debt
– a trauma he never forgot.

The Blacking Factory
(right) The bitter experience
of working here as a boy was
to scar Dickens for life.

imagination with ghoulish tales of the occult and of the horrors told her by the midwife and undertaker.

But at this time it seemed as if 'everything was happy'. Not even Dickens' first school – kept by a 'grim and unsympathetic old personage, flavoured with musty dry lavender and dressed in black crape', who 'ruled the world with the birch' – could cloud these idyllic days.

Unable to join in the games of his companions because of his frail physique, Dickens found happiness in reading. 'When I think of it, the picture always arises in my mind of a summer evening, the boys playing in the churchyard, and I sitting on my bed, reading as if for life.'

Together with a love of reading, Dickens delighted in singing, mimicry and recitation. He began performing at home to selected guests, then his proud and boastful father took him to local inns, where, standing on a stool or table, he sang comic songs, or recited short stories learned by heart, for which he would 'be tipped' and treated to a dinner of 'salmon and fowl'.

Acting and entertaining certainly seemed to come more easily to him than scholarship. Dickens disliked school. And the type of school to which he was sent became the subject of his lashing satire, instilling in him a lingering revulsion for the Bible-thumping, kill-joy views of the puritans of his day. To him they were selfish, vain, spiteful and ill-tempered – qualities that he despised above all others.

But school made less of a lasting impression on him than the Kent countryside, the Kent coast and the towns of Rochester and Chatham. Like young Pip in *Great Expectations*, he explored the Kent marshes – that "dark flat wilderness beyond the church" – and at Chatham docks saw prisoners from the prison hulks manacled together.

PAIN AND POVERTY

In 1822, when Charles was ten, the Dickens family moved yet again – to 16 Bayham Street, Camden Town, in London. John Dickens' debts had become so severe that all the household goods were sold, and reduced circumstances and the demands of a growing family left no money to educate Charles.

The family's fortunes plummeted to still greater depths. Mrs Dickens had the desperate and somewhat impractical idea of bolstering their income by starting a school, and so rented a house at 4 Gower Street North, in the more fashionable – and expensive – area of Bloomsbury. The brass plate '*Mrs Dickens' Establishment*' adorned the door, but Dickens later recorded that 'Nobody ever came to the school, nor do I recollect that anybody ever prepared to come . . .'

Unable to pay his debts, John Dickens was taken to the Marshalsea, the debtors' prison, where he was later joined by his wife and children. Two weeks earlier, two days after his twelfth birthday, Dickens had begun work at Warren's Blacking Factory – wrapping shoe-blacking bottles for six shillings a week. It was

Key Dates

1812 born at Landport, near Portsmouth
1817 moves to Chatham, Kent
1822 moves to London
1824 works at Warren's Blacking Warehouse
1828 enters journalism
1830 falls in love with Maria Beadnell
1833 first story published. Breaks with Maria Beadnell
1836 *Sketches by Boz* published. Marries Catherine Hogarth
1837 first child born. Moves to Doughty Street. Mary Hogarth dies
1839 moves to Devonshire Terrace
1842 visits America
1851 father dies. Moves to Tavistock House
1856 buys Gad's Hill
1857 meets Ellen Ternan
1858 first public reading. Separation from Catherine Dickens
1863 mother dies
1865 visits France with Ellen and Mrs Ternan
1867 American reading tour
1870 dies at Gad's Hill

possibly the most traumatic event of his life, and certainly he felt that it was the most shameful. Virtually nobody knew, until his death in 1870, that Dickens had worked at Warren's, an experience he called 'the secret agony of my soul'.

Some six months later, the family's fortunes revived – a small inheritance paid off most of the debts – and the Dickens family emerged from prison. Charles' father removed him from Warren's, although his mother felt that it might be better for him to stay on. Charles never forgave her.

The awful experience at Warren's had a profound effect on Dickens. His obsessive determination never to be short of money, and his stringent attitude to household management (he partly blamed his mother's mismanagement for his father's imprisonment) had their roots in his response to this experience of 'shameful' poverty. His compassion for poor, abused, abandoned children probably originated here, too.

SCHOOLDAYS AND YOUTH

Having removed his son from the warehouse, John Dickens sent him to a nearby private school, Wellington House Academy ('Salem House' in his fictionalized autobiography, *David Copperfield*). A fellow pupil said of him, 'My recollection . . . is of a rather short, jolly-looking youth, very fresh-coloured, and full of fun, and given to laugh immoderately without any apparent reason . . . He was not particularly studious, nor did he show any special signs of ability.'

Three years later, aged 15, Dickens left Wellington House and, through his mother, was found a job as office boy to a firm of solicitors (Ellis & Blackmore) in Gray's Inn. The work was dull and undemanding, but the pay was enough for him to become acquainted with London life. In the music-halls and theatres of the 1820s, Dickens saw at first-hand the young bloods, pimps, prostitutes, drunkards and other examples of low life that were to people his first attempts at fiction.

But he was not happy with the law and had no intention of remaining a clerk all his life, so with a copy of Gurney's *Brachygraphy*, he began teaching him-

Dickens House Museum

Barnaby's Picture Library

48 Doughty Street
(left) Now a Dickens Museum, this was the author's home from 1837-9, where he enjoyed both public acclaim and domestic contentment, and wrote The Pickwick Papers, Oliver Twist *and* Nicholas Nickleby. *His sister-in-law Mary formed part of the household soon after Dickens' marriage to Catherine Hogarth; she was his ardent admirer and companion until her tragically early death in 1837.*

Dickens House Museum

self shorthand, thinking of journalism as a career. He quickly mastered the discipline.

After a brief period with another solicitor, Charles Molloy in Lincoln's Inn, Dickens started work as a freelance reporter in Doctor's Commons – the court where church and nautical cases were heard, and marriage licences to 'love-sick couples and divorces from unfaithful ones', were granted. His contempt for the law was confirmed but, with a ticket to the Reading Room of the British Museum, he set about educating himself. The time spent here, he was later to say, was the most useful of his life.

FIRST LOVE

Now 18, Dickens fell in love with Maria Beadnell, the pretty, bright-eyed daughter of a Lombard Street banker. For four years he courted her, while she, though enjoying his attention, flirted and gossiped and toyed with him, finally snubbing him at his twenty-first birthday party (which he paid for himself), by calling him 'boy' and then leaving early. Heart-broken, Dickens returned her letters.

Few were to know of the pain the affair caused him. Only in middle-age, when he met her again, 'toothless, fat, old and ugly', did he finally exorcise her ghost – though he remained resentful and disillusioned.

Although this event damaged his pride and self-esteem, he had already become one of the foremost reporters of his day. Joining the *Mirror of Parliament* – which reported verbatim on the daily proceedings of Parliament – in 1832, he also contributed to an evening paper, the *True Sun*.

But, just as familiarity with the law had bred contempt, so insights into the workings of the House of Commons and 'honourable' Members of Parliament led to a profound detestation. In his experience, most MPs were 'pompous', with only 'a tolerable command of sentences with no meaning in them'.

Joining the liberal *Morning Chronicle* (second only to *The Times* in circulation), Dickens reported on the nationwide meetings that led to the great Reform Act of 1832. In the days before railways and the telephone, Dickens had to take his copy to London by coach, and it was always a race to see whether he or *The Times* man would file his story first. It was an exciting and heady experience, but though journalism was to remain a lasting passion, it was an anonymous short story that started Dickens' rise to fame.

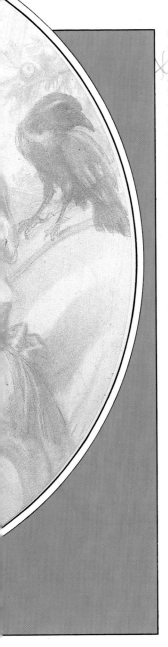

Dickens' children
(above) Kate, Walter, Charles and Mary – shown here in 1841 – were the first four of nine surviving children.

Catherine Dickens
(left) Cruelly rejected by Maria Beadnell, Dickens later courted and married Kate Hogarth, whom he often affectionately addressed in his letters as 'dearest darling Pig'. The match met with approval on all sides, especially since Catherine's father, a journalist himself, recognized and appreciated the young Dickens' talents.

THE ORIGINS OF MISS HAVISHAM

Miss Havisham, in *Great Expectations*, seems a rather far-fetched figure but Dickens may well have based her on real characters. When Dickens was a boy, a weird old lady, dressed in white, was often to be seen wandering aimlessly near London's Oxford Street. This potent image was reinforced by a report published in *Household Words* in 1850. This told the story of Martha Joaquim, whose lover blew his brains out while sitting next to her: 'From that instant she lost her reason ... led the life of a recluse, dressed in white and never going out'.

Wilkie Collins' novel, *The Woman in White* – 'the very title of titles', said Dickens – was published just three months before *Great Expectations*. Evidently, the conundrum of these mad women, arrested in time by the traumatic loss of a lover, and dressed in white caught and held Dickens' imagination.

Fitzwilliam Museum, Cambridge

Roy Miles Fine Paintings/Bridgeman Art Library

Wilkie Collins
(above) A lengthy correspondence between Dickens and his fellow-author led to the choice of Collins' most famous title, The Woman in White.

The jilted bride
(left) Victims of dashed hopes and unrequited love, real-life women in white haunted Dickens' imagination and inspired the creation of the weird Miss Havisham.

Entitled by the publishers 'A Dinner at Poplar Walk', Dickens' first published story appeared in the *Monthly Magazine* in 1833. Though he received no payment for the piece, he was asked to contribute more. Seizing the opportunity, Dickens wrote a series of 'sketches' under the pen-name of 'Boz' (his youngest brother Augustus' nickname). Under the same name, he also contributed short pieces of fiction and reviews to the *Morning Chronicle* and the *Evening Chronicle*, for which he received two guineas a piece in addition to his salary. From these modest beginnings, Dickens' career as a writer took off rapidly. His collected stories were published on his twenty-fourth birthday, in 1836 – under the title *Sketches by Boz*.

SUCCESS AND MARRIAGE

With the money he made from *Sketches by Boz*, and a commission to write 20 monthly instalments of 12,000 words (*The Pickwick Papers*), Dickens felt financially able to marry. On 2 April, 1836, he married Catherine Hogarth, the placid, voluptuous daughter of George Hogarth, the editor of the *Evening Chronicle*.

The marriage lasted until 1858 (when the couple separated) and produced 10 children (one of whom died). It had all the outward signs of happiness and contentment, but was not what Dickens had hoped for.

But in 1837, with the birth of his first son and the publication of *The Pickwick Papers*, which sold 40,000 copies a week, the future looked bright. The young author was fêted everywhere. He commanded a large income, from both his fiction and his journalism.

At his new home, 48 Doughty Street, he lived the life of a gentleman in a household that included his brother, Fred, and his wife's sister, Mary, who at the age of 16 came to keep house.

Dickens developed a strong attachment for Mary, and she for him. To him, she seemed everything that his wife was not – quick, intelligent, and interested in all that he did. When, in May 1837, Mary became ill and died (in his arms), Dickens felt that he had been dealt a blow from which he would never recover. She, or an idealized vision of her, was to remain with him, appearing in his novels as Rose Maylie (*Oliver Twist*),

Gad's Hill
(above) John Dickens pointed out this house to young Charles, saying that it might one day be his. Dickens bought it in 1856.

A tribute to success
(right) Spy's sketch of Dickens was made in 1870 – the year of his death – from memory.

WIFE AND MISTRESS

Secret guilt tormented Dickens' later years. His wife, Catherine, was a placid and amiable woman but her disorganization and vacuity infuriated him. Agonizing over marital responsibilities and his own ingratitude, his health began to fail.

Dickens' life changed when he met Ellen Ternan, a well-born actress, in 1857. His passion for her led him to re-evaluate his jaded marriage, finding it 'a dismal failure'. At the inevitable separation, he claimed that Catherine was an unfit wife and mother which led to an acrimonious public row. But when Catherine left, her sister Georgiana remained in the marital home, confusing the gossips. Surprisingly, the scandal did little to harm Dickens' popularity.

Dickens never openly declared his love for Ellen but she was a frequent visitor to Gad's Hill. She accompanied him to France – with her mother – and he rented a house for her, with lodgings for himself nearby. It was Ellen who was called to his deathbed and named first in his will.

Dickens House Museum

Mrs Catherine Dickens *in later life. She and Charles separated in 1858.*

Dickens House Museum

Ellen Ternan, *the young actress whose friendship with Dickens lasted until his death.*

Poet's Corner
(right Despite Dickens' contempt for pomp, his grandiose tomb at Westminster Abbey places him among the titans of literature.

By courtesy of the Trustees of the Victoria and Albert Museum

Little Nell (*The Old Curiosity Shop*) and Little Dorrit. His sense of loss led Dickens to view the love between brother and sister as the perfect kind.

ILLNESS AND NOSTALGIA

During the long years spent with Catherine (1836–1858), Dickens achieved the status of the greatest living writer of his day. Despite being plagued by ill-health – suffering from rheumatism of the face, a congenital kidney complaint and a weak heart – his creative energy was boundless. In addition to 10 major novels written during these years and numerous short stories (including the celebrated *A Christmas Carol*), he edited a popu-

lar weekly (*Household Words*), started a new national daily newspaper and worked in various charities.

In 1856, Dickens took a step that reunited him with the past. Gad's Hill Place in Kent was a house his father had pointed out to him when he was a boy, saying that it might one day be his when he was rich and famous. Now, rich and famous, he bought the house. After separation from Catherine in 1858, he lived there until his death in 1870.

A year before leaving his wife, Dickens fell in love with a mysterious young actress, Ellen Ternan – mysterious because even now little is known of her or of her life with Dickens. However, the extraordinary lengths to which the couple went to hide their relationship would seem to indicate that they were lovers.

From 1858 onwards, despite recurrent bouts of illness, Dickens threw himself into a series of remarkable public readings of his works to rapturous audiences. He toured England, Scotland, Ireland and the United States, to which he returned in 1867–8.

Prompted partly by financial necessity, the readings gave Dickens the thrill of the footlights, of acting, and of being able to move an audience to both laughter and tears, but it was a punishing programme.

Prematurely aged, and unable to pronounce even the name 'Pickwick', Dickens returned to Gad's Hill Place in 1870. On 8 June he spent the day working on his latest novel, *Edwin Drood*. That evening he collapsed, and the next day he died.

Dickens left a fortune of £93,000 – more than half of which came from the proceeds of his public readings. He was buried, against his wishes, in Westminster Abbey, amid the pomp and ceremony of a system he had spent his life attacking. Two days after his death, Queen Victoria voiced the feelings of many. 'He is a very great loss', she confided to her diary. 'He had a large loving mind and the strongest sympathy for the poorer classes.'

Magnificent Performer

Dickens crammed his waking hours with work to assuage his increasing sense of dissatisfaction. But his fame was such that he was obliged to live out his personal tragedies in the glare of publicity.

The image which Dickens had carefully fostered for many years of a man happy only in the bosom of his family was no more than that – an image. Despite his having written movingly of the joys of marital bliss, his own marriage, after the early years, had been a torment. The only solace he had found or would ever find was through an almost manic activity. 'I have no relief', he wrote to his old friend John Forster, 'but in action. I am incapable of rest. I am quite confident I should rust, break and die, if I spared myself. Much better to die, doing.'

Nor did he spare himself. Apart from being a highly acclaimed and prolific author, he was a dedicated journalist, an implacable social reformer, an inveterate traveller and increasingly, as compensation for his domestic problems, an intense and expressive actor/stage manager.

Dickens had entered journalism at the age of 16 in 1828, when he joined the *Mirror of Parliament*, a transcript of the proceedings of Parliament. In four years of relentless hard work, his speed, efficiency and determination 'lifted me up into that newspaper life, and floated me away over a hundred men's heads'. But it was not until he started *Household Words* in 1850 that he found an instrument capable of expressing his ideas, personality and consummate skill as an editor. This weekly journal of some 20,000 words contained a varied, enter-

Full of promise
The handsome young Dickens is pictured right at the age of 27 – three years married, the father of a son and the successful contributor to several publications. He had already achieved overnight fame with his first novel, Pickwick Papers.

Holiday haven
(below) Dickens found Broadstairs in Kent to be such a pleasant resort that he holidayed there every year but two between 1837 and 1851. It was most conducive to writing (except when the street musicians drove him to despair), and he worked here on Pickwick Papers *and* David Copperfield.

Youthful bride
When Dickens married Catherine Hogarth (left) in 1826 she was just 20 years old, with a gentle, amiable disposition. But Catherine's charm and prettiness were to lose their appeal for Dickens, as he felt increasingly the lack of an intellectual soul-mate. He addressed the same problem in fiction, not least through the character of his semi-autobiographical hero, David Copperfield.

Weidenfeld Archives

Star reporter
'I have worn my knees by writing on them in the old gallery of the old House of Commons' (right), wrote Dickens, who made his mark reporting Parliamentary debates. Exceptionally young for the job, he was acclaimed by a colleague as having 'occupied the very highest rank, not merely for accuracy in reporting but for marvellous quickness in transcript'. In fact another said of him, 'There never was such a shorthand writer!'

D. Maclise: Charles Dickens/Tate Gallery on loan to National Portrait Gallery, London

ment. This was hard for some readers to swallow, but both the principles and the popularity of *Household Words* continued unimpaired. Dickens' most uncompromising novel to date, *Hard Times*, a savage indictment of Victorian materialism, was serialized in *Household Words* and doubled sales in ten weeks.

The day to day running of the magazine was left to the sub-editor, William Henry Wills, but Dickens himself took on the responsibility for planning each issue, commissioning articles, reading and rewriting copy, correcting proofs and finding new authors. Wherever he went, at home or abroad, he always received his weekly package of articles and proofs sent by Wills for him to read and approve. With characteristic determination, he stamped his personality and views on every page.

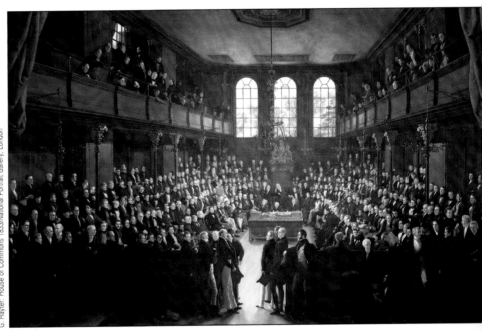

G. Hayter: House of Commons 1833/National Portrait Gallery, London

taining and educative mixture of fiction and hard-hitting articles exposing and attacking Government and Establishment corruption. Though it was directed at a mass market, Dickens cautioned contributors not to be patronizing. 'Don't think', he warned them, 'that it is necessary to write *down* to any part of our audience.'

Dickens published his own fiction in *Household Words*, as well as that of other distinguished writers. They included the young and hitherto unknown Wilkie Collins, Mrs. Gaskell, Edward Bulwer-Lytton (once famous for his historical novels such as *The Last Days of Pompeii*) and Charles Reade (who was so highly regarded at the time that he was hailed by many as Dickens' natural successor as a novelist). The paper took up the cause of social reform, championing workers' rights, campaigning for better housing and sanitation and popularizing the scientific and technical achievements of the day. One of the radical stands taken in *Household Words* was that working men have a right to form trade unions, and that together they should challenge the 'Indifferents and Incapables' of Parlia-

Nothing was published of which he did not approve, nor any view expressed with which he did not agree. No contributor was credited by name, and Dickens' name alone appeared on the title page.

Household Words ran successfully for nine years until Dickens fell out with its publishers. He pointed out that they might need him, but he did not need them. And to prove the point, he immediately started another weekly magazine called *All the Year Round*. It was an instant success, its circulation far outstripping that of *Household Words* to reach an amazing 300,000. The new magazine followed the same formula as that of *Household Words*, and its pages contain much of Dickens' sharpest social criticism. But an important innovation in *All the Year Round* was that a serialized story by a well-known writer occupied a key position at the beginning of the journal. Dickens began in grand style with his own *A Tale of Two Cities*, following this with another immensely popular work, Wilkie Collins' *The Woman in White*.

Dickens' output was prodigious in the 1850s,

for his fictional writings did not lag behind his journalism. *Little Dorrit* alone amounted to over 380,000 words and was written over 18 months concurrently with his dictation of the 125,000 words of *A Child's History of England*. Yet even this intense literary activity was not a sufficient outlet for his superabundant energy, and acting increasingly provided a further distraction and emotional release.

Dickens' love of the theatre had always been strong. Had writing not claimed him, he said, the theatre would almost certainly have done so. Acting became the means by which he was able to express publicly aspects of his personality he felt unable to communicate either to his wife or, because of the rigidity of Victorian conventions,

Lifelong champion
(right) The literary and dramatic critic John Forster was a rude, overbearing and argumentative man, but one who dedicated himself to those writers he admired. Dickens met him in 1836 and they established an immediate rapport. Forster was to be Dickens' longest held, most deeply valued friend and his most fervent champion.

Victoria and Albert Museum, London/Weidenfeld Archives

D. Maclise R.A.
Friday 22ᵗ May: 1840.

Dickens House Museum

Kate and Mary
Dickens is pictured left with his beloved daughters Katey and 'Mamie' in about 1865. When the family split, Mary was loyal to her father and even ended a love affair on his advice. Hot-headed Kate, known as "Tinderbox", stayed at Gad's Hill under protest, and married to get away from its unhappy atmosphere.

'Aunt Georgy'
Catherine's young sister, Georgina (painted right by Dickens' brilliant friend Daniel Maclise) became a central member of the household. She remained at Gad's Hill after the marital breakdown – something which gave rise to lurid gossip.

D. Maclise Girl at the waterfall/Victoria and Albert Museum, London

had only served to entrench the differences of character between his wife, Catherine, and himself. Her indolent, winsome disposition, which had enchanted him as a young man, came increasingly to infuriate him. And, like David Copperfield, who was tied to the sweet but helpless Dora, Dickens was haunted by the 'one happiness I have missed in life, and one friend and companion I have never made'.

He was painfully aware that his demanding, dominating nature accentuated the peevishness and passivity of Catherine's – and vice versa. And he confided to Forster the sad truth that 'Poor Catherine and I are not made for each other, and there is no help for it. It is not only that she makes me uneasy and unhappy, but that I make her so too . . . I am often cut to the heart by thinking what a pity it is, for her sake, that I ever fell in her way . . .' but 'nothing on earth could make her understand me, or suit us to each other . . .'

No satisfactory way out presented itself, but the need for one became paramount when Dickens fell impetuously and romantically in love with Ellen Ternan. His attentions to her were for the time being platonic, but Catherine, under pressure from her family, left Dickens.

So began a bitter public wrangle between Dickens and his supporters, and Catherine and her family. Georgina, Catherine's sister, stood by Dickens, and insisted on remaining in the Dickens home, where for years she had taken Catherine's place as housekeeper and mentor to the children. Rumour now linked Dickens' name with his sister-in-law as well as Ellen, and he felt impelled to

Müller: Piazza San Marco, Venice, with a procession/Bridgeman Art Library

to anyone else. In no play was this tendency of self-dramatization more obvious than in Wilkie Collins' melodrama *The Frozen Deep*.

The play, first produced at Dickens' London home, Tavistock House, on Twelfth Night, 6 January 1857, was almost a prophecy of the unhappiness which was soon to engulf his own life. The story concerned two Arctic explorers, Richard Wardour and Frank Aldersley, both in love with Clara Burnham. Wardour, the rejected suitor, saves the life of his rival, though in so doing he dies in the arms of Clara. Taking the part of Wardour, Dickens poured out all his frustrated longing for love and understanding, all his pent-up desire for a soul-mate. So convincingly did he play the part that his fellow actors were reduced to tears.

It was decided to stage the play in Manchester. Before an audience of 3,000, Dickens' performance was, Wilkie Collins reported, a 'magnificent piece of acting. He literally electrified the audience'. But the staging was to have unforeseen consequences. In place of his daughters, Mamie and Katey, and the other lady amateurs, Dickens engaged professional actresses, Mrs Ternan and her daughters, Ellen and Maria. Though 18-year-old Ellen took only a minor role on stage, she was to play a major part in Dickens' life.

The production of *The Frozen Deep* coincided with a crisis point in Dickens' marriage. The years

Venetian visions

"The wildest visions of the Arabian Nights are nothing to the Piazza of Saint Mark [above] . . . the gorgeous and wonderful reality of Venice, is beyond the fancy of the wildest dreamer. Opium couldn't build such a place." Thus wrote Dickens when a tour of France and Italy in 1845 took him to Venice for the first time. Overwrought from writing The Chimes, *and full of nervous energy, he left London with a lust for activity and new sights.*

SPONTANEOUS COMBUSTION

The awful fate of Krook in *Bleak House* leaves only charred bones and a "sickening oil". In the Preface Dickens wrote of 30 other such cases "on record", and clearly believed in the phenomenon. Others mocked, as in this cartoon.

Victoria and Albert Museum, London

publish impassioned and probably unwise statements of the innocence of all slandered parties, including himself.

The storm of separation was weathered with pain and difficulty, and from 1859 Dickens made Gad's Hill in Kent his permanent base. His relationship with Ellen Ternan continued, and although they never lived together openly, Dickens set Ellen up with a house in Peckham, south London. She became his lover, though not the soul-mate he craved, for their differences of age, background, experience and intelligence proved too great to bridge. At Gad's Hill he had his daughters, Mamie and the fiery Katey, for company. But Katey, who had sided with her mother in the separation, was so miserable that she finally agreed to marry Wilkie Collins' younger brother, Charles, whom she did not love. Dickens thought this ill-advised, but was forced to accept the match. After Katey had departed on her honeymoon, he buried his face in her wedding-dress, and wept, 'But for me, [she] would not have left home.' Now only Mamie and the ever-faithful 'Aunt Georgy' remained in residence at Gad's Hill.

AN ELECTRIFIED AUDIENCE

At the height of the scandal over his marriage, Dickens had undertaken a series of public readings of his work throughout Great Britain. He had already severed relations with some of his oldest friends, and it was highly uncertain how a public fed on a diet of Victorian morals would react. But Dickens' ability to 'electrify' an audience remained unshaken. In Ireland, the men cried even more unashamedly than the women; and the Edinburgh reading was a triumph – 'The Chimes shook it; Little Dombey blew it up'; every night women begged for the flower from his buttonhole; the halls were jam-packed; and in a month he made over 1,000 guineas profit.

From then until his death in 1870, Dickens undertook several major reading tours, both in Britain and the United States. They provided him with much needed income for the upkeep of Gad's Hill and the support of his children, and gave him immense emotional satisfaction. Each reading was a resounding success, as he terrified his audiences with the murder of Nancy, or moved them to tears with the death of Little Nell. On one occasion he made even the austere critic Thomas Carlyle laugh uncontrollably with the 'Trial from Pickwick'. He told Dickens, 'Charley, you carry a whole company under your hat'.

But the physical strain was enormous, causing him both nervous exhaustion and worrying symptoms of ill health. His left cheek began twitching, his foot swelled to such a size that he was unable to wear a shoe or walk, and he suffered pains in his stomach and chest. Yet he refused to let up. In the last 12 years of his life he undertook 450 paid performances, netted over £45,000 – almost half his final estate – and made such an impression upon his audience that many were to recall his performances years after his death.

A talented gathering
Dickens' Household Words *helped to make famous such up-and-coming writers as Wilkie Collins (shown heavily bearded on Dickens' left).*

While his popularity was greater than ever before, his personal life continued to be unsatisfactory. The separation from Catherine did not bring him the happiness he had sought or the love he craved, though he was possibly less unhappy. His relationship with Ellen Ternan, always a closely guarded secret, brought as much strain as any relief

Stage-struck
Dickens could well have made a career in the theatre, for while he was still in his teens he had such a reputation as an amateur actor that he was invited to audition for a professional part. Below he is seen in one of his most famous roles, the boastful, cowardly soldier Bobadill in Ben Jonson's Every Man in His Humour. *It was through his theatrical work that he met and fell in love with actress Ellen Ternan (left).*

it gave him. Work, as always, proved the greater satisfaction.

And in the work of these last years, in both the novels and the journalism, there is a greater depth, as well as a more bitter sense of contemporary malaise. England was 'on the downward road to being conquered' and seemed 'content to bear it and would NOT be saved'. The ruling class – the aristocracy and commercial middle class – was corrupt, caring for nothing but its own comfort. Greed, self-interest and small-minded patriotism characterized the age. Only from the working man did Dickens hold out any hope of a proper 'discharge of electoral responsibilities more seriously for the common good than the bumptious singers of "Rule Britannia".'

CREATIVE TO THE END

His nine children also failed to fulfil the high hopes he had of them. 'All his fame', said a friend, 'goes for nothing, since he has not the one thing [he desires]. He is very unhappy in his children.' Of his seven sons only Henry proved a success, despite his father's doubts about his chosen path – Cambridge and the Law. But he continued to love them all and be anxious for their well-being.

Dickens returned from his American reading tour of 1868 broken in health. Despite this, after a short rest the old energy and restlessness returned. He embarked upon a series of 12 'farewell' readings, completing them only days before his death. He began another book, *The Mystery of Edwin Drood*, destined never to be finished; but the sales of the first six episodes, 'very, very far outstripped

Whistle-stop tour
(above) Scotching rumours that his second trip to America was a rest cure, Dickens embarked on a gruelling schedule of public readings. Rushing from venue to venue by train took its toll. The carriages were so hot that he often resorted to the aft-platform, where "it snows and blows, and the train bumps and the steam flies at me, until I am driven in again." The tour was a resounding success, but the strain of it ruined his health.

every one of its predecessors'. It showed that he still possessed enormous creative powers, for in spite of his prolific output there were few signs of repetition or staleness.

Dickens died of a stroke at Gad's Hill while hard at work on *Edwin Drood*. So he ended his life as he had lived it – an uncompromising artist. The news of his death caused worldwide sorrow. The American poet Henry Longfellow wrote to Forster, 'I never knew an author's death to cause such general mourning . . . this whole country is stricken with grief.' In London, thousands flocked to Dickens' tomb at Westminster Abbey, which was left open for two days after the funeral, and strewed it with flowers. He himself had once written, 'Whoever is devoted to an Art must be content to deliver himself wholly up to it, and to find recompense in it.' No better epitaph for Dickens could have been written.

$\bigcirc$ *Fact or Fiction* $\bigcirc$

A TALE OF TWO MEN

When Dickens undertook *A Tale of Two Cities,* his most valuable source of information was *The French Revolution* (1837), by his friend Thomas Carlyle (right). Their books have much in common. Before starting work, Carlyle read 'till he was full of his subject', Dickens until the Revolution took 'complete possession' of him. Both books were written under acute stress – Dickens' just after the break-up of his marriage, Carlyle's when he was facing penury.

For both men, the work represented a personal risk. If Carlyle's book failed, he vowed to give up writing, buy a spade and rifle, and go to the American Frontier. Dickens' very peace of mind depended on achieving a masterpiece faithful to his intent, for he hoped by it to exorcize his mental anguish. Their fears of failure, however, proved groundless: *A Tale of Two Cities* raised the circulation of Dickens' new periodical *All the Year Round* to 40,000 copies a week; and Carlyle's 'prose epic' made his reputation as a historian, and remains the most famous book on the subject.

A TALE OF TWO CITIES

In this, his only historical novel, Dickens intertwines the lives and fortunes of innocent individuals with the political and social changes sweeping France.

Inspired by Carlyle's history of the French Revolution, *A Tale of Two Cities* is a chilling and dramatic account of the mounting tension in France of the 1770s and '80s, and the explosive rebellion of the French people against their aristocratic oppressors. It is also a human story about individuals caught up in the turmoil, and the two aspects of the novel are woven together with what has been described as 'exquisite construction'. The subject is harrowing, the pace is relentless, emotions run high – *A Tale of Two Cities* is a gripping story that cannot fail to enthral.

GUIDE TO THE PLOT

The individual drama concerns Lucie Manette, a young Frenchwoman brought up in England. Her father – whom she believed to be dead – has been released from prison, where he has been incarcerated for 18 years. Dr Manette has been given into the care of Monsieur Defarge, his former servant and now the owner of a wine-shop in the Saint Antoine suburb of Paris. Lucie and Jarvis Lorry, an official of Tellson's Bank, London, go to Paris to bring the doctor back to England and Lucie pledges to restore her father's frail hold on life through her redeeming love.

Five years later, in 1780, Mr Lorry, Lucie and Dr Manette are reluctant witnesses at an Old Bailey trial. A young man,

Charles Darnay, is accused of treason for the aid he has supposedly given to "Lewis, the French King, in his wars against our said serene, illustrious, excellent, and so forth . . ." But since the case is based on a question of identification, the trial collapses when one of the lawyers, Sydney Carton, draws attention to the great physical similarity between himself and the accused. Carton appears to be a wastrel, unlike the gentlemanly and sober Darnay.

On a quiet street in London, Lucie has established a happy household into which Jarvis Lorry, Charles Darnay, Sydney Carton and another lawyer, Mr Stryver, now come as friends. It would be an idyllic establishment were it not marred by shadows from Dr Manette's past and by premonitions of disruption to come.

In France tensions are increasing. Outrages continue against the poor, who begin to retaliate. The Marquis St Evrémonde is murdered, and his nephew, none other than Charles Darnay, becomes the inheritor of 'a system that is frightful to [him]'. Meanwhile, Charles has declared his love for Lucie. So too do Stryver and Carton. Charles is the favoured suitor, but Sydney Carton pledges his devotion to Lucie and all her loved ones. Despite earlier protestations that he cared for no-one, and no-one cared for him, his apparent cynicism hides more profound and worthy

"The golden thread"

(right) Doctor Manette, released after 18 years in the Bastille, is gradually restored to an active, pleasurable life by the care of his daughter, Lucie. But he is still haunted by memories of his imprisonment, and then "only his daughter had the power of charming this black brooding from his mind."

Eaton Gallery, London/Bridgeman

De Troy: The Oyster Lunch/Musée Condé, Chantilly/Lauros Giraudon Bridgeman

feelings: "I wish you to know that you have been the last dream of my soul . . . I would embrace any sacrifice for you and for those dear to you."

At the wine-shop in Paris, the awesomely composed Madame Defarge watches all, sits knitting, and compiling a register of those to be dealt with when the time is right. Remorseless and inexorable, she sustains those around her with the thought that though they have waited a long time, retribution for the people against their oppressors is steadily approaching: "When the time comes, let loose a tiger and a devil; but wait for the time with the tiger and the devil chained

"Monseigneur was about to take his chocolate. Monseigneur could swallow a great many things with ease, and was by some few sullen minds supposed to be rather rapidly swallowing France."

Louvre, Paris/Bridgeman

In the wine-shop
(above) Here the implacable Monsieur and Madame Defarge draw together the earliest elements of revolution – represented by the "three Jacques".

Sharp contrasts
(left and below right) France is dominated by an aristocracy who are "exquisite gentlemen of the finest breeding" – but totally indifferent to any interests other than their own. They swallow up all that the poor can produce, as they toil to pay "the tax for the state, the tax for the church, the tax for the lord". But even so humble a figure as a mender of roads plays his own small part in fuelling the fires of political change.

– not shown – yet always ready."

On the morning of his marriage to Lucie, Charles reveals to Dr Manette his true, aristocratic identity. The shock of this news causes the doctor to suffer a nervous collapse. For nine days he recognizes no-one. He reverts to the "old scared lost" behaviour he displayed in his imprisonment, and to his occupation of that time – shoemaking.

It is now 1789. "Every pulse and heart in Saint Antoine was on high-fever strain and at high-fever heat." Arms are being given out and Madame Defarge has abandoned her knitting for an axe. The Bastille is taken.

Three years later, with the nobility scattered, Charles receives a letter from his servant Gabelle, whom he had left in

Sydney Carton *works at night to perform legal "miracles" in the Old Bailey the next day. In court he meets the Manettes.*

charge of his unwanted inheritance. Despite having administered the estate with humanity, Gabelle is in prison and he begs Charles to rescue him. Telling no-one of his intentions, Charles sets off for Paris, leaving letters for Lucie and Dr Manette.

On entering Paris, Charles' aristocratic identity is discovered and he is arrested and imprisoned in the Conciergerie. A few days later, Dr Manette and a distraught Lucie appear at Tellson's Bank in Paris, where Mr Lorry is trying to sort out his French clients' affairs. Mr Lorry urges the Doctor to use his influence with the people to find Charles immediately. Outside, the

Joseph Vernet: Construction of a road (detail)/Louvre, Paris/ courtesy of Giraudon/Bridgeman

mob has gone mad – they are sharpening their weapons at the grindstone and murdering their prisoners. Meanwhile the Defarges visit Lucie and her family, and cast a great shadow, "threatening and dark", over them. To Lucie's pleas for mercy, Madame Defarge replies, "All our lives we have seen our sister-women suffer . . . Is it likely that the trouble of one wife and mother would be much to us now?" Dr Manette, however, finds Charles and keeps contact with him, though he cannot effect his release. Fifteen months pass during which time the violence and bloodshed increase and "The sharp female newly-born, and called La Guillotine" is never idle.

At last Charles is brought to trial, and, largely on the testimony of Dr Manette, he is freed. However, his triumph is brief and he is retaken that night – fresh evidence has been brought against him.

A chance meeting between Miss Pross (Lucie's companion), Jerry Cruncher (odd-job man at Tellson's), John Barsad (a spy with access to the Conciergerie prisoners) and Sydney Carton gives Carton the means of committing Barsad to a promise: if it should go ill with the prisoner, Carton will be allowed to visit him once. Carton has a grim plan which he develops during the course of a long sleepless night.

The new evidence is unanswerable and Charles is condemned to death. Worse still, Madame Defarge is also intending to charge both Lucie and her father. Sydney Carton now prepares his plan to save Charles and engineer the escape of the whole family, thinking 'It is a far, far better thing that I do, than I have ever done . . .'

A DRAMATIC HISTORY

'It has been one of my hopes to add something to the popular and picturesque means of understanding that terrible time,' said Charles Dickens of his intentions in writing *A Tale of Two Cities*. So successful was he at portraying 'that terrible time' that, after the exuberant exaggeration and comic invention of his earlier works, the Victorian critics found fault with this historical novel for being too sombre and lacking in humour.

A Tale of Two Cities begins with a grim account of pre-Revolutionary France. It is the year 1775 – 'It was the best of times, it was the worst of times'. It was a time of extremes, of polarization between rich and poor, when violence and inhumanity ruled and life was held cheap. From the outset, the ironic tone chills as it mocks. In the name of Christianity, France "*entertained herself . . . with such humane achieve-*

> "*O Miss Manette . . . when you see your own bright beauty springing up anew at your feet, think now and then that there is a man who would give his life, to keep a life you love beside you!*"

ments as sentencing a youth to have his hands cut off, his tongue torn out with pincers, and his body burned alive, because he had not kneeled down in the rain to do honour to a dirty procession of monks . . ."

In every sentence, in every step of the plot, the horror of the times is revealed. All imaginative deviation, entertaining sub-plot, and even ordinary dialogue are kept to a minimum to allow the story to forge ahead. The two comic characters, Miss Pross and Jerry Cruncher, are not principally created to entertain – each is

J. J. Zoffany: Plunder of the King's Wine Cellar 10 August 1792/Noorton Brod Gallery, London/Bridgeman

Mary Evans Picture Library

Under the plane-tree
(above) Lucie and her father's quiet home in Soho attracts their old friend Mr Lorry, and two new ones: Charles Darnay and Sydney Carton.

A reprisal
The brutal Marquis St Evrémonde is murdered. The message from Jacques reads: "Drive him fast to his tomb."

essential to the functioning of the plot. Like the Revolution itself, that slowly at first, then more quickly gained purpose and momentum, the novel gathers pace and complexity with each turn of events.

It is written on two levels – the national and individual. Dickens is concerned to give us insights into the minds of both oppressors and oppressed, and into the direct links of cause and effect between the crushing system of the *ancien régime* (old order) and the violent excesses of the mob. The hanging of "old Foulon" is an example of such violence:

"*Down, and up, and head foremost on the steps of the building; now, on his knees; now, on his feet; now, on his back, dragged, and struck at, and stifled by the bunches of grass and straw that were thrust into his face by hundreds of hands; torn, bruised, panting, bleeding, yet always entreating and beseeching for mercy . . .*"
Horrific as such incidents are, they are

Roy Miles Fine Painting, London/Bridgeman

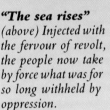

"The sea rises"
(above) Injected with the fervour of revolt, the people now take by force what was for so long withheld by oppression.

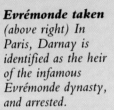

Evrémonde taken
(above right) In Paris, Darnay is identified as the heir of the infamous Evrémonde dynasty, and arrested.

clearly the result of long years of oppression by a brutal and capricious aristocracy.

As *A Tale of Two Cities* weaves back and forward between Paris and London we are drawn into the complexity and anguish of the individual drama. On the one hand, Charles Darnay, as a represen-

tative of his class and his particular family, is an oppressor, but personally his fault is minimal. Even Dr Manette, hero of the people because of his long period of suffering, is not immune, and would have stood accused against the people had Madame Defarge not been thwarted.

LIFE AND DEATH

Central to *A Tale of Two Cities* is the theme of death and renewal. On both the historical and individual levels of the novel, Dickens presents his case that out of death can come life.

"Recalled to life" is the disconcerting message delivered to Mr Lorry early in the story. As the mystery slowly unravels, we learn that he who has been virtually buried alive for 18 years has been "recalled to life". It is not simply his release from prison that is to restore Dr Manette to life, however. The power to heal his deranged mind comes from the restorative love of his daughter Lucie, whose tender soul is tortured by the idea that she unwittingly neglected her father for many years, believing him to be dead. Once given the opportunity, she loses no time in becoming "the golden thread that united him to a Past beyond his misery, and to a Present beyond his misery".

LOVE AND DEVOTION

Lucie herself attracts love and devotion from all who come into close contact with her. Her companion, Miss Pross, "with the vigorous tenacity of love, always so much stronger than hate", is able to rout Madame Defarge, who is committed to the idea of Lucie's destruction. Out of Madame Defarge's death comes safety not only for the Manettes but for all those who might have become the victims of her pitiless nature.

For love of Lucie, Sydney Carton undertakes to "embrace any sacrifice for [her] and for those dear to [her]". When the time comes, he faces his sacrifice with selfless courage, and is transformed from a wastrel into a man of true nobility.

On the historical level, too, the theme of death and renewal is played out. The atrocities perpetuated against the people gave birth to an equally fearsome and vengeful mob. But out of these two evils, Dickens, attributing the prophetic vision to Carton, looks forward to *'a beautiful city and a brilliant people rising from this abyss, and, in their struggles to be truly free, in their triumphs and defeats, through long years to come, I see the evil of this time and of the previous time of which this is the natural birth, gradually making expiation for itself and wearing out.'*

| In the Background |

THE GUILLOTINE

The guillotine, first used in 1792, was introduced to make execution as painless and humane as possible. It takes its name from the physician Joseph Ignace Guillotin, who pressed for the law requiring the death sentence to be carried out by a machine. Previously, execution by beheading (using an axe) had been a 'privilege' only of the aristocracy.

Bibliothèque Nationale, Paris/Bridgeman

CHARACTERS IN FOCUS

In *A Tale of Two Cities*, Dickens created a tightly-knit group of characters "whom the story shall express, more than they should express themselves by dialogue". Their subtleties emerge through involvement with each other and with external events. So the pathos of Dr Manette's past, or the complexity of Sydney Carton's position are conveyed with powerful economy.

WHO'S WHO

Sydney Carton An astute barrister and self-styled "dissolute dog", whose unprepossessing appearance and manner make him an unlikely hero.

Lucie Manette Disparaged by Carton as "a golden-haired doll", she secretly inspires his devotion.

Doctor Manette One-time inmate of the Bastille, he rediscovers through Lucie a life of charmed content – but echoes still reach him from his painful past.

Charles Darnay In England, an inoffensive young French tutor; in France, a hated aristocrat.

Jarvis Lorry "A mere man of business", his charm, sense and gentleness endear him to Darnay and the Manettes.

Mr Stryver A bumptious barrister, "shouldering" his way to a "large and lucrative practice".

Monsieur the Marquis St Evrémonde Darnay's uncle, whose name is "more detested than any name in France".

Monsieur Defarge "Good-humoured-looking . . . but implacable-looking too", the former servant of Dr Manette plays a major part in the Revolution.

Madame Defarge More relentless than her husband, her path is to cross with the Evrémonde family, through "the emigrant", Darnay.

Miss Pross A "wild, red woman", she is Lucie's devoted slave, fiercely jealous of her "hundreds" of suitors.

Lucie Manette (right) is the most devoted of daughters, with a genius for creating domestic happiness. She inspires love in all who come to know her – including such disparate characters as Darnay, Carton and Stryver. In her house, "everything turned upon her, and revolved about her." Marriage and motherhood only increase the charmed circle around her, and enhance the gift that Darnay describes as "your being everything to all of us, as if there were only one of us, yet never seeming to be hurried or to have too much to do . . ."

Madame Defarge (left) has been "imbued from her childhood with a brooding sense of wrong, and an inveterate hatred of a class . . . She was absolutely without pity." She inspires awe even in her husband and the vengeful Jacques Three who frequents her wine-shop. Daily she knits into her fateful register the names of all those who have wronged the people. Defarge says, "It would be easier for the weakest poltroon that lives, to erase himself from existence, than to erase one letter of his name or crimes from the knitted register of Madame Defarge."

"Idlest and most unpromising of men", Sydney Carton (right) is brought face to face with his good "other self" when he meets Charles Darnay, whom he instantly dislikes because – as he says to himself – ". . . he shows you what you have fallen away from, and what you might have been!" His "half-insolent manner", heavy drinking and ironical speech are all designed to make bearable the knowledge that he has wasted his life, a knowledge which nevertheless "eats him away". But his silent, self-denying love for Lucie rekindles his true sensitivity and generosity of spirit.

"Doctor Manette (below), intellectual of face and upright of bearing", regains his old energy and sense of purpose in the company of his long-lost daughter. "He studied much, slept little . . . and was equally cheerful", and gives an impression far removed from the pathetic, lost figure reclaimed from the Bastille. But the ghost of that time has still to be laid . . .

Mr Lorry (right) of Tellson's Bank (London and Paris), is a neat, efficient bachelor, devoted to his work. Under the little brown wig he wears, are "a pair of moist bright eyes" that he must have been at "some pains to drill to the composed and reserved expression of Tellson's Bank". His solitary life is cheered by the Manettes. When Lucie gets married, he tells her, "You leave your good father, my dear, in hands as earnest and loving as your own."

Charles Darnay's "condition was that of a gentleman" (left). A self-possessed and honourable young man, he seeks to establish a quiet, industrious life in London with his beloved Lucie, his daughter (another Lucie) and Dr Manette. His fate, however, is to be the sole surviving heir of the Evrémonde family, who represent in France the essence of class oppression. He renounces his property, saying, "it is a crumbling tower of waste, mismanagement, extortion, debt, mortgage, oppression, hunger, nakedness, and suffering." But he risks his own safety, and that of his family, by returning to Paris at the height of the Revolution to attempt the rescue of his faithful servant, Gabelle.

THE SUPREME STORYTELLER

Dickens' eye for detail and eccentricity fired the imagination of his audience. His gift lay in creating characters who have become 'the friends of all mankind'.

Dickens was the most popular novelist of his day. For almost 35 years, until 1870, he dominated the English literary landscape. Read by virtually everyone who could read, his novels – published for the most part in monthly or weekly instalments – were eagerly awaited by all sections of society.

The effect his writing had on his audience was sensational. Even the hard-headed Scots philosopher, Thomas Carlyle, implored him not to kill off Little Nell in *The Old Curiosity Shop,* because it would be too much for him to bear. And when Dickens did just that, Daniel O'Connell, the Irish Nationalist MP, who happened to be reading it in a railway carriage (Dickens' books were sold on station bookstalls), flung his copy out of the window, crying, 'He should not have killed her', before breaking down and sobbing.

AN URGE TO REFORM

The impetus for Dickens' vast output – short stories, plays, reviews, newspaper articles, travel books, childrens' books and 14 major novels – can be seen as the 'one common end', described in *Dombey and Son:* 'To make the world a better place'.

Personal experience of childhood injustice, and compassion for the plight of London's poor were the mainsprings of Dickens' art, and were to stay with him throughout his life. It was said that his face would 'blaze' with indignation at a tale of social outrage – his stories and publications put his deepest convictions into words.

While it is debatable whether he instigated any of the social reforms enacted by Parliament in his lifetime – and they were many and various – his writing could, on occasion, have direct and practical results. As a chronicler of low life, and as a champion of the poor, the weak and the lonely, Dickens could affect individuals and institutions alike.

With the express intention of moving people to do something about the plight of the poor in England, Dickens wrote *The Chimes* and *A Christmas Carol* before Christmas 1843 and 1844 respectively. And Dickens succeeded in this aim because of his captivat-

ing, almost hypnotic powers as a storyteller. Always a very visual writer, taking delight in describing sights and sounds and the feel of things, and lavishing detail upon detail, he rarely failed to move even the hardest hearts.

After reading these Christmas stories the young Robert Louis Stevenson wrote, 'I have cried my eyes out, and had a terrible fight not to sob. But, oh dear God, they are *good* – I feel so good after them – I shall do good and lose no time – I want to go out and comfort someone – I *shall* give money. Oh, what a jolly thing it is for a man to have written books like these and just filled people's hearts with pity.'

But the world that Dickens writes about is not simply one of social injustice and human misery. It is also a world of sunlit days and Christmas dinners; a world of merrymaking and goodwill; a world of lovable eccentrics such as the naive adventurer Mr Pickwick, and the ever-optimistic, but ever-impecunious Mr Micawber. And in telling his stories, Dickens created a fascinating and complex world of the imagination in which real passions are unleashed and difficult moral dilemmas explored.

Christmas cheer
(left) This festive illustration from A Christmas Carol *epitomizes a major facet of Dickens' world – the revelry, fellowship and goodwill associated with Christmas.*

"So very 'umble"
(right) The repeated mannerism of wringing his hands while asserting that he is "so very 'umble" makes Uriah Heep – the fawning, scheming clerk in David Copperfield *– one of Dickens' unforgettably malevolent characters.*

Dickens' Dream
(left) This unfinished painting shows Dickens dozing in his Gad's Hill study – which is teeming with characters from his imagination.

Serialized stories
(right) Dickens' novels were published in serial form – mostly in monthly instalments. Great Expectations appeared weekly.

Family readings
(below) Each episode was eagerly awaited, and often read aloud by one of the family.

Dickens was a dedicated writer from the very beginning of his career. Often rising and bathing in cold water before seven, he disciplined himself to his task in a way few other writers have equalled. Once he had started, which was not always easy, and got 'his steam up', he would go at it 'tooth and nail', sometimes working until three in the morning.

LIVING CREATIONS

During these solitary hours of labour, he entered into a never-never land where the characters and creations of his teeming mind became so vivid and intense that they acquired a reality of their own. He certainly spoke of them in everyday conversation as if they were real. And when the time came to dispose of them within the story, he talked of having to 'kill them off', of 'murdering them' and 'doing them in'. If he had the power of making others cry at his creations, he also wept openly when writing a sad scene. He delayed writing about the death of Little Nell for two weeks because he found the anguish too great.

Dickens lived the characters he created. His daughter Mary recalls how he would frequently leap up from his desk, run to a mirror and mouth sentences into it as if he were acting a part. And with the passing of time he came to look on himself as 'a fond parent

Brian Gibb/Topham Picture Library

The writing chalet

(above) Dickens had this Swiss chalet erected in his garden at Gad's Hill as a refuge for writing. It was after a day spent working here that he died.

to every child of my fancy' and declared that 'no one can ever love that family as dearly as I love them'.

The love and vitality which Dickens bestowed on his characters are echoed by the affection and vividness with which the reader remembers them. Dickens focuses on idiosyncrasies of speech, dress and appearance, and often gives his characters repeated 'stock phrases' which virtually sum them up and certainly commit them to memory. In *David Copperfield*, the persistent Barkis is always "willin' " (to marry Peggotty), while the cringing, scheming clerk Uriah Heep is "so very 'umble".

HUMOUR AND SATIRE

Having a very acute ear for turns of phrase, Dickens used such speech patterns as a source of humour in all his works – but he also used them as a vehicle for satire. With Mr Chadband in *Bleak House,* Dickens ridicules the ranting style of nonconformist preachers. "What is peace?" he asks rhetorically. "Is it war? No. Is it strife? No." Continuing this meaningless tirade, Chadband exposes both his own absurdity and the self-interested pomposity of 'Christians' of his kind.

Yet it is not just Dickens' knack of capturing personality in a single phrase that makes his characters memorable. The mark of his genius lies in his gift for giving them a compelling power and psychological authenticity. Uriah Heep haunts the pages of *David Copperfield* with insidious malevolence, while Miss Havisham in *Great Expectations* is the personification of dashed hopes and embittered

revenge. In a world of such imaginative power, even the impossible is believable; the gin-soaked rag-and-bone man Krook in *Bleak House* literally bursts into flames with 'spontaneous combustion', consumed by greed, suspicion and malice.

Names themselves mattered enormously to Dickens and his manuscripts testify to the effort that went into choosing them. The names he chose often conveyed personal or moral traits – from Mr Bumble, the incompetent beadle who runs the workhouse in *Oliver Twist,* to the austere Mr Gradgrind, the no-nonsense schoolmaster intent on extinguishing his pupils' imaginations in *Hard Times*. It comes as no surprise that the abominable Wackford Squeers in *Nicholas Nickleby* believes in the liberal use of the birch.

A MUTUAL UNDERSTANDING

Sometimes Dickens uses the first person (the narrator as 'I') to tell the story, as in *David Copperfield* and *Great Expectations*. It is no coincidence that these are also the most directly autobiographical of all his major novels.

But in most cases he is the author telling the story, talking directly to his audience. In *The Chimes,* he acknowledges this role and says, "it is desirable that a story-teller and a story-reader should establish a mutual understanding as soon as possible".

In this respect, Dickens gained from being published in serial form – it gave him the ideal opportunity to establish a 'mutual understanding' with his readers. Careful to arrange the plot so that each instalment ended on a

'cliff-hanger', serialization also allowed him room for improvisation and alteration in response to his readers' reactions.

Dickens' relationship with his readers remained of prime importance to him. His public readings, which began in 1858, recalled the early, rapturous success he had had in print. Despite the exhaustion that the performances caused him, he wrote 'the people lift me out of this directly; I find that I have quite

Weidenfeld and Nicholson

Public readings

(left and above) Dickens loved to perform public readings of his works. One of his favourites was the scene in Oliver Twist *where Nancy is murdered by Sikes. Audience response helped him to keep in touch with what his readers most enjoyed.*

forgotten everything but them and the book in a quarter of an hour'.

Dickens' public also lifted him out of the poverty of his early years, although financial security was be no means immediate. *The Pickwick Papers* sold 40,000 copies a month after a slow start, and was to be surpassed only by the sales of his last, unfinished story, *The Mystery of Edwin Drood,* which sold some 100,000 copies an episode. At the height of his fame Dickens wrote an insignificant short story entitled *George Silverman's Explanation,* for which he was paid the unprecedented sum of £1,000. But despite his financial success, Dickens never lost his integrity.

Dickens' stories create a picture of the writer very similar to that described by George Orwell. Behind the pages of Dickens, Orwell saw 'the face of a man who is always fighting against something, but who fights in the open and is not frightened, the face of a man who is generously angry . . . a type hated with equal hatred by all the smelly little orthodoxies which are now contending for our souls'.

A prolific writer of immense literary stature, Dickens merits a special place in *The Great Writers*. Here is an illustrated sampler of his most popular fiction up to 1848. His writing career began in 1833 with articles and short stories in periodicals, these later appearing in *Sketches by "Boz"*.

The early success of *The Pickwick Papers* (1837) led to his first serialized novels – *Oliver Twist* (1837), *Nicholas Nickleby* (1839) and *The Old Curiosity Shop* (1841).

The hugely popular *A Christmas Carol* (1843) was first in a series of four seasonal Christmas tales. *Dombey and Son* (1848) is renowned as the first work of Dickens' mature genius, marking a point of departure into subtler psychological explorations and a wider social panorama.

Mary Evans Picture Library

Arthur Rackham, courtesy of Barbara Edwards/Mary Evans Picture Library

A CHRISTMAS CAROL

◆ 1843 ◆

Ebenezer Scrooge (left), visited on Christmas Eve by the shackled ghost of his dead business-partner Marley, has been the subject of modern interpretations from cartoons to Christmas cards. This vivid little story of the grumpy, ill-natured old miser frightened out of his selfishness by visions of his future doom has caught the imagination of generations of readers. For many people the story has come to define Dickens. The sweet-tempered lame boy, Tiny Tim, and his bullied father, Bob Cratchit (above), are the very picture of courage and cheer in adversity, just as Scrooge himself is the epitome of meanness. With its eerie Christmas ghosts and the resounding goodwill of its ending, this enchanting tale remains a seasonal classic.

A Christmas Carol became the first of a series of Christmas books, all with happy endings, now available in collected editions. *The Chimes* (1844) built on the success of the first story and was followed by *The Cricket on the Hearth* (1845), *The Battle of Life* (1846) and, finally, by *The Haunted Man* (1848).

OLIVER TWIST

✦ 1837 ✦

Oliver, (right and below) a penniless orphan drawn into London's criminal underworld, is the focus of Dickens' first real novel. A gripping tale of murder and intrigue, the book also carries a powerful invective against the treatment of poor children by Victorian society. Grotesquely comic scenes are set against unforgettable dramatic episodes – such as Oliver's introduction to Fagin's gang, the murder of Nancy and the pursuit of Bill Sikes. The study of Fagin in the condemned cell explores another of Dickens' life-long fascinations – the workings of the criminal mind. Dickens deeply resented the charge that the book glamorized crime.

THE PICKWICK PAPERS

✦ 1837 ✦

Mr Pickwick, (left) with his gaiters and spectacles, is one of Dickens' most famous comic creations. With the other members of the Corresponding Society of the Pickwick Club – Tracy Tupman, Nathaniel Winkle and Augustus Snodgrass – Samuel Pickwick becomes involved in a series of hilarious and heart-warming adventures, reports of which make up this delightful book. Sam Weller, appearing as Mr Pickwick's servant in the fourth instalment, contributes his shrewd cockney wit to forge a comic combination unrivalled in Victorian literature.

More connected than *Sketches by Boz*, but still loose in structure – constructed simply in the form of a series of incidents – *The Pickwick Papers* allowed Dickens to give free rein to his love of characterization. We meet the tricky Job Trotter and his quick-witted master Alfred Jingle; the greedy pious Mr Stiggins and the bizarre Mrs Leo Hunter. *The Pickwick Papers* was hugely popular when published and is now quite unjustly neglected.

R.B. Martineau: Kit's Writing Lesson/ Tate Gallery, London

THE OLD CURIOSITY SHOP
→ 1841 ←

Little Nell, (Nell Trent) (above) lives in the old curiosity shop with her grandfather. The wicked moneylender Daniel Quilp seizes their shop, and the poverty and hardship they endure kills the young girl. Nell and her devoted admirer Kit are two of Dickens' most sentimental creations, and although Victorian readers wept openly at Nell's death scene, the tear-jerking pathos may be a little too much for 20th-century taste. But Quilp is a magnificent creation of pure evil – this sadistic, twisted dwarf haunts the reader long after the happy ending (Kit's marriage) has been forgotten.

DOMBEY AND SON
→ 1848 ←

Florence Dombey (below) is the rejected heroine of _Dealings with the Firm of Dombey and Son,_ which opens with the 'Son' in question being born to the cold, arrogant businessman Mr Paul Dombey. The boy's mother dies giving birth, and Dombey focuses all his hopes on his son and heir Paul, neglecting his devoted daughter Florence. But little Paul dies in childhood. Dombey decides to marry again to obtain another heir, choosing the imperious widow Edith Granger for his wife. This contract is arranged by Dombey's manager James Carker, who has his own plans for Edith. Despite Dombey's power, he loses everything – except Florence. In _Dombey and Son,_ Dickens examines the facade of middle-class respectability, and achieves a new emotional depth.

W. Maw Egley: Flo Dombey/Victoria and Albert Museum/Bridgeman Art Library

NICHOLAS NICKLEBY
→ 1839 ←

Nicholas (left) is the high-spirited hero of one of Dickens' funniest novels, which is packed with incident, tension and biting satire. When Nicholas – incensed by the cruel practices at Dotheboys Hall – thrashes the headmaster Wackford Squeers, he is acting out Dickens' hatred of all those who maltreat children. Escaping from the school with the defenceless, half-witted Smike, Nicholas joins a group of travelling actors before returning to London where his uncle plots his downfall. The benevolence of the effusive actor-manager Vincent Crummles and the kindly Cheeryble twins highlight the wickedness of Squeers and Nicholas' uncle Ralph (later prescribed the death penalty by Dickens).

The French Revolution

Mixing high ideals with violent mob rule, the French Revolution transformed every aspect of French society, sent shock waves throughout Europe and inspired Dickens' great historical novel.

A Tale of Two Cities is unique among Dickens' works in being set (at least partly) in a foreign country and dealing with a great historical event. It is not surprising, however, that the French Revolution should appeal to Dickens' imagination because it was an event of such gripping human drama as well as being of huge importance in European – indeed, world – history.

In opening his book with the memorable words "It was the best of times, it was the worst of times", Dickens expressed some of the strongly ambivalent feelings that the Revolution was to arouse, for although the bloodshed appalled tender minds, the famous ideals of liberty, equality and fraternity

The palace at Versailles
Ironically, this supreme embodiment of royal status was also to be the scene of the States General that marked the beginning of the Revolution.

remained an inspiration to liberal thinkers throughout the 19th century.

The Revolution spanned ten years, from 1789 to 1799. It involved an extremely complex series of events, but in essence it represented an attack on the privileges and abuses of the ruling classes. Trouble had been brewing for some time before things finally came to a head in 1789. Louis XIV, whose enormously long reign stretched from 1643 to 1715, gave the monarchy a power and prestige unmatched elsewhere, but his personal glory disguised serious weaknesses in the state that were to haunt his successors.

The reign of Louis XV (1715-74) was marked by a series of disastrous wars which left France weakened and divided. When the young Louis XVI became king in 1774 he was in theory an absolute monarch – that is, one with no constitutional limits to his power. Just as he claimed absolute temporal

Réunion des musées nationaux, Versailles/Bridgeman

Musée Carnavalet, Paris/Jean-Loup Charmet

Crushing taxes

(left) The Church and Aristocracy add to the already prostrating weight of taxes on the poor in this 1789 cartoon. The attitude of many aristocrats is summed up by Dickens' Marquis St Evrémonde: "Repression is the only lasting philosophy. The dark deference of fear and slavery . . . will keep the dogs obedient to the whip . . . I will die, perpetuating the system under which I have lived."

power over his subjects, so the Catholic Church maintained that it had spiritual sovereignty over them. Most of these subjects were peasants working the land, and as such they were both legally and economically tied to the aristocracy. They had virtually no rights, nor freedom of any kind. Little seemed to have changed since the feudal order of the Middle Ages.

In practice, however, things were different. Louis XVI was popular with his subjects but was a weak character. He had little control over his ministers, who often pursued contradictory policies, and even less over the country as a whole. The Church was also losing its hold over the population, a significant part of which despised its worldliness and wealth. And there was widespread resentment towards the clergy and the aristocracy. France had been suffering serious inflation since the 1730s, yet the richest classes were exempt from taxation.

The economic situation had been aggravated — and royal prestige considerably damaged — by the

Musée de Versailles, France/Bridgeman

Poverty and privilege

Louis XVI and his queen Marie-Antoinette (above) were the figureheads of the pre-Revolutionary social and political system. Louis was not a cruel man but he had a dull mind and little understanding of the needs of the poor. In the painting at left he is depicted distributing alms during the terrible winter of 1788. His portly, richly dressed figure stands out strangely in the miserable scene. As he was to discover, charity was an inadequate substitute for the social reform that was needed.

Bulloz

series of wars in Louis XV's reign, during which France lost Canada and most of its possessions in India. And although France successfully helped the American colonists in their struggle for independence against the British, this served to highlight the contrast between the ideals of liberty and democracy across the Atlantic and the perpetuation of privilege and repression at home.

There was little need to import democratic ideology from America, however, for in this period – which has become known as the Age of Enlightenment – progressive thinkers looked to reason, not traditional values, to solve the problems of human affairs. The finest minds in France were virtually unanimous in their criticism of the existing order. Philosophers like Denis Diderot and Voltaire, whose names have become practically synonymous with the Enlightenment, mocked the old order, with its myriad injustices, and urged the adoption of constitutional reforms on British lines. And the enormously influential Jean-Jacques Rousseau,

who believed in the natural goodness of mankind, put forward a theory of the State in which sovereignty would rest in the general will of the whole nation.

Matters were brought to a head in the late 1780s by a catastrophic financial crisis. The king's finances were so shaky that in 1787 he tried to impose taxes on the privileged classes, but they refused to pay. The next year there was a disastrous harvest followed by an exceptionally harsh winter, and the miseries of the poor intensified the sense of a divided nation. It was clear that a complete monetary reform was needed, and Louis took the extreme step of summoning the States (or Estates) General (*Etats-Généraux*), a body that had not met since 1614.

CALLS FOR REFORM

The States General was a representative assembly that could be called by the king to deal with major matters of state. It was made up of representatives of the three 'estates' or orders of the realm: the Church was the First Estate; the aristocracy was the Second Estate; and the Third Estate was made up of the remaining 95 per cent of the population. The States General met at Versailles on 5 May 1789. Each of the three estates presented grievances to the king, and it became clear that major social and political reforms, far exceeding Louis' immediate financial objectives, were expected.

The members of the Third Estate refused to submit to their 'superiors' in the clergy and aristocracy. They represented not only peasants, but also members of a growing middle class that was frustrated by its lack of political power. On 17 June the deputies of the Third Estate defiantly proclaimed

A new constitution
The self-appointed National Assembly, composed of the more radical members of the States General – mostly the representatives of the Third Estate – took the famous 'Tennis Court Oath' at Versailles on 20 June 1789 (above). They then set themselves to forging a new constitution, using the American Declaration of Independence as a model. A contemporary cartoon shows one member of each estate represented in the Assembly hard at work, literally "hammering it out" (inset). The new constitution listed citizens' rights and limited those of the king, although there was at this stage no intention to abolish the monarchy.

themselves the National Assembly and pledged to end feudal privileges. They were joined in this by a good many clergymen and a few aristocrats. The king ordered their meeting-place to be closed, but they adjourned to an indoor tennis court, and on 20 June swore an oath not to disband until France had been given a constitution.

Louis yielded one week later and legalized the National Assembly. At the same time, however, he summoned troops to Versailles. This was a dangerous move, and on 11 July he made a grave misjudgement when he allowed himself to be persuaded by a court faction to dismiss his finance minister, Jacques Necker, a highly popular figure. This sparked off an insurrection in Paris, and on 14 July one of the most famous events in French history took place – the storming of the Bastille. A mob attacked this ancient prison in Paris because it was seen as a symbol of the king's absolute power. To many contemporaries, as well as to later writers, this was the true beginning of the Revolution, and July 14 – Bastille Day – is still a national holiday in France.

The storming of the Bastille prompted outbursts of rioting throughout France, as peasants pillaged and burned aristocrats' châteaux. This spasm of violence became known as the Great Fear (*Grande Peur*), and an English traveller, Arthur Young, who was passing through Besançon on 27 July, wrote: 'Many châteaux have been burnt, others plundered, the seigneurs hunted down like wild beasts, their wives and daughters ravished, their papers and titles burnt and all their property destroyed.'

To escape the carnage many aristocrats fled the country, and on 4 August 1789 the nobles and

beginning of the French Revolutionary Wars, in which France fought various European powers. (The wars lasted until 1802, then resumed in 1803 as the Napoleonic Wars).

At first things went badly for France in the war, and rumours of royal treason led a mob to storm the Tuileries Palace, where the king was living, on 10 August 1792. Louis was imprisoned and a revolutionary government – the Commune – replaced the legally elected one. Many royalist sympathizers were arrested, and between the 2nd and 6th of September mobs throughout France entered prisons and slaughtered hundreds of prisoners (the 'September massacres'). The Commune replaced the Legislative Assembly with the National Convention, which at its first meeting on 21 September abolished the monarchy.

Louis was put on trial as a traitor and was executed on 21 January 1793. Britain, until then neutral, joined the coalition of foreign powers at war against France, and a royalist revolt broke out in the Vendée, in the west of the country. With civil war tearing the country apart and the prospect of being overrun by the coalition powers, France was in acute crisis. The Convention surrendered its powers to the Jacobins, who established an emergency government directed by the Committee of Public Safety, created on 6 April 1793.

THE REIGN OF TERROR

The aim of the Committee was to galvanize national resistance in the face of threats from abroad and to stamp out all internal counter-revolutionary elements, and in less than a year it had driven foreign armies from France, defeated the royalist forces in the Vendée, and stabilized the economy.

A terrible price was paid for the stabilizing effect of the Committee of Public Safety, however, for in the desire to rid the country of all treasonable elements, thousands of people were imprisoned or executed – Marie-Antoinette was guillotined on 16 October 1793. The period from June 1793 to July 1794 is known as the Reign of Terror, when it is estimated that some 40,000 people were executed throughout France.

The fall of Robespierre in 1794, who had dominated the Committee of Public Safety in late 1793, marked the end of the Terror. In 1795 a new constitution came into force under which executive power was held by a board of five Directors, and the period from then until 1799 is known as the Directory. France in this time lurched from one crisis to another. Order was restored by the young Napoleon Bonaparte. In 1799 he returned to France from his campaign in Egypt, at the age of 30 a national hero for his brilliant feats as a soldier. On 9 November, with the support of the army and several government officials, he overthrew the Directory and established in its place the Consulate, whereby the country was governed by three Consuls, of which he was clearly the most dominant. In all except name he was now ruler of France. The French Revolution had come to an end, but France had been irrevocably transformed.

clergy in the Assembly relinquished their privileges, destroying France's feudal structure at a stroke. On 26 August the Assembly adopted the Declaration of the Rights of Man and Citizen, a document – much indebted to the American Declaration of Independence – that listed the 'inalienable rights' of the individual, including those of 'liberty, property, security, and resistance to oppression'.

There were rumours of a counter-revolutionary royalist plot, and on 5 October a mob from Paris marched on Versailles and forced the King and his Queen to move to the capital, where they lived as virtual prisoners of the Revolution.

THE KING FLEES PARIS

In 1791 the Assembly completed its constitution, giving the king limited power. Louis decided that his best chance of restoring the old order was to join those of his nobles who had fled abroad and raise foreign aid, and on 20-21 June 1791 he tried to leave the country. His plan failed, however, and he was captured at Varennes, about 100 miles from Paris. Reluctantly, the king accepted the constitution, and the National Assembly terminated its own existence of 30 September 1791.

On 1 October the National Assembly was replaced by the Legislative Assembly, a new national parliament. Its members were drawn mainly from the various political clubs of Paris, of which the best known were the Girondins and the Jacobins. One of the most pressing matters concerning them was the threat of invasion from Austria, for rumours were rife that Marie-Antoinette (who was Austrian by birth) was plotting with the court in Vienna. On 20 April 1792 war was declared on Austria, and this marked the

Storming the Bastille
(above) Blue-coated French Guards join forces with the revolutionaries to attack this ancient fortress and prison, a hated symbol of the despotism of the Bourbons. This triumph is celebrated annually on July 14th, 'Bastille Day', a French national holiday with parades, fireworks and speeches. The key to the Bastille was sent by the people of France to George Washington.

Bibliothèque Nationale, Paris/Jean-Loup Charmet

GREAT EXPECTATIONS

Full of tingling twists, vivid images, violence and sentimentality, this is one of Dickens' most popular novels. Echoing his childhood memories, it explores a grand theme — how to know yourself.

The first few pages of *Great Expectations* contain one of the most startling and dramatic openings to be found in any classic novel. Spellbinding in its intensity, it leads the reader – at a furious pace – into a vivid portrayal of childhood fears and anxieties, rich in humour and sorrow alike. An irrepressible enthusiasm for people and places, examples of rattling dialogue or gripping action are to be found on almost every page. Weirdly eccentric, awesomely 'threatening and colourfully comic characters are plentiful.

A GUIDE TO THE PLOT

Dickens locates the early part of the story in the bleak marsh country of the North Kent coast, set in the period of his own childhood there. It is a desolate landscape, described as "raw", "leaden" and "savage". The central character and 'storyteller' is Pip, a sensitive orphan brought up by his bullying older sister and his gentle foster-father and loyal friend, Joe Gargery the blacksmith.

One cold Christmas Eve towards nightfall, young Pip visits the graves of his dead family in the overgrown churchyard. He is "growing afraid of it all and beginning to cry" when the desolation is abruptly shattered by the terrifying Magwitch, a convict escaped from the Hulks. Under threat of being eaten alive and having his liver cut out, Pip is terrified into stealing food, drink and a file from home. The next day he witnesses the prisoner's recapture and, although his own crime is never discovered, his guilt is complete.

The following autumn Pip receives a strange invitation to wait on the pleasure of a rich and eccentric lady in the local town, Miss Havisham. A "ghost" of a woman deserted by her lover on her wedding day, Miss Havisham lives in a state of perpetual grief in her crumbling mansion, dressed in a yellowing wedding dress.

There Pip meets Estella, a beautiful orphan being raised by Miss Havisham to be an instrument of revenge upon the male sex. Pip, however, becomes infatuated with her, and her contempt only makes him feel bitterly ashamed of his own inadequacies and lowly station in life.

The convict in the churchyard
(left) Young Pip's first encounter with the terrifying Magwitch is one of the most compelling opening chapters ever written. His threats of cannibalism set the scene for recurrent images of violence.

Awaiting an outcome
(right) Pip's mysterious fortune is dispensed by the awesomely powerful lawyer Jaggers. The anxiety that accompanies 'great expectations' is eloquently evoked in this study, painted in 1857.

Prison hulks at Portsmouth
(above) *Dilapidated vessels crammed with felons "like a wicked Noah's Ark", haunt the bleak, "leaden" landscape of Pip's youth.*

Pip and Estella
(right) *Haughty and beautiful Estella fires Pip's fervour to become 'a gentleman'. She taunts him with the truth—he is "a common labouring-boy" — yet he loves her.*

Pip's regular visits cease after ten months when he is apprenticed to Joe at the forge, Miss Havisham providing his master with 25 guineas as payment for his indentures. Four years later, nursing a growing resentment at his lot, Pip suddenly learns that he is the beneficiary of a mysterious patron, has "great expectations", and is to be educated in London as a "gentleman". He believes, understandably, that he owes it all to Miss Havisham, and that she has plans for him and Estella to be married.

Pip duly goes to London and soon becomes a dreadful snob, disdainfully neglecting his childhood friends. But despite appearances he is far from happy in his idle, hedonistic lifestyle. Becoming a London gentleman only entails acquiring an accent, clothes, servants, entertainment and money. But the dispensation of his fortune is left in the hands of Jaggers, an awesome lawyer whose trade is deception and the perversion of true justice.

Continually snubbed by Estella, by now an attractive young woman, Pip's rejection of friends, foster-family and background blinds him to his failings and the values of the world to which he aspires.

> "*In the little world in which children have their existence whosoever brings them up, there is nothing so finely perceived and so finely felt, as injustice. It may be only small injustice that the child can be exposed to; but the child is small, and its world is small …*"

Increasingly isolated and alone, Pip grows disillusioned with the false glitter of London society. But he feels that his education, manners and wealth have cut him off from his childhood friends, Joe and Biddy. Thus begins the real story of *Great Expectations* – Pip's search for his true identity. Who he really is can only be learned when he discovers the identity of his mysterious benefactor.

Like all masters of the mystery story, Dickens keeps his readers guessing. With Pip, the reader is led down a series of false trails, and made to make false assumptions based upon misleading circumstantial evidence. When, finally, his secret benefactor is revealed, it

In Jaggers' assistant Wemmick, Dickens combines two views of the human condition. Wemmick has the split personality of a man who personifies an inhuman legal system while at work, but in the privacy of his "Castle" and the company of his "Aged Parent" displays a true sense of the ridiculous. Thus, in Chapter 55 Pip witnesses an unconventional event that typifies Wemmick's comic side in its very private capacity.

. . . I was considerably surprised to see Wemmick take up a fishing-rod, and put it over his shoulder. 'Why, we are not going fishing!' said I. 'No,' said Wemmick, 'but I like to walk with one'.

I thought this odd; however, I said nothing, and we set off. We went towards Camberwell Green, and when we were thereabouts, Wemmick said suddenly: 'Halloa! Here's a church!'

There was nothing very surprising in that: but again, I was rather surprised, when he said, as if he were animated by a brilliant idea: 'Let's go in!'

We went in, Wemmick leaving his fishing-rod in the porch, and looked all round. In the mean time, Wemmick was diving into his coat-pockets, and getting something out of paper there.

'Halloa!' said he. 'Here's a couple of pair of gloves! Let's put 'em on!'

As the gloves were white kid gloves, and as the

An orphan's impression of family

(left) Cooling churchyard, Kent – setting for the dramatic opening. The letters on his parents' tombstones suggest to Pip "a square, stout, dark" father and a "freckled and sickly" mother. That Dickens reduced the number of "lozenges" to five shows his concern for credibility.

comes as a shock not only to Pip, but also to the unsuspecting reader – though Dickens was careful to have sown enough clues for the revelation to be convincing.

Pip's discovery leads him into a nightmare world full of soul-searching psychological drama packed with action and danger. Struggling with life and death issues, Pip finally learns his lesson, expunges his guilt, and retrieves his childhood 'inner' self.

GROTESQUE COMEDY

Dickens thought of *Great Expectations* as a 'grotesque tragi-comic conception'. The tragedy – Pip's tragedy – is that he follows falsehood and becomes a snob. The way in which Miss Havisham rejects human fellowship and becomes cynical and bitter, using Estella to wreak revenge upon men, is also tragic. But, as in almost all that Dickens wrote, the tragedy is relieved by a wonderful sense of humour and a comic vein that courses through the book. Writing to his friend and agent John Forster, Dickens said that in creating the characters of Pip and Joe he had 'put a child and a good-natured foolish man in relations that seem . . . very funny'.

In the Background

TRANSPORTED FOR LIFE

From 1776 to 1787, violent criminals such as Magwitch were crammed into floating hulks like those haunting the landscape of Pip's childhood. Eventually England rid itself of those who survived by shipping them to Australia – the penalty for returning was death. Gradually wheat and sheep, and the discovery of gold, transformed the hostile forests and hills of Australia into a land of opportunity. Convicts escaped or were rehabilitated, freed and given land. Transportation was finally abolished in 1868.

post-office was widened to its utmost extent, I now began to have my strong suspicions. They were strengthened into certainty when I beheld the Aged enter a door escorting a lady.

'Halloa!' said Wemmick. 'Here's Miss Skiffins! Let's have a wedding.'

After the dramatic change in Pip's life and the gloom of Newgate prison – both of which take place in the previous chapter – Wemmick's wedding seems like a scene from a fairy tale. The analogy is apt in another way; *Great Expectations* can be read as a fairy tale, but one in which the 'rules' change.

True to the fairy tale tradition, Pip dreams of becoming a prince charming. His dream comes true through, he thinks, the intervention of his fairy-godmother, Miss Havisham. Pip hopes to marry his princess, Estella, in the belief that together they will live happily ever after.

> "So, throughout life, our worst weaknesses and meannesses are usually committed for the sake of the people whom we most despise."

The Aged Parent
(right) One of Dickens' most cheerful characters, Wemmick's Aged Parent is always "in great spirits", and is "as proud as Punch" of his son's "pretty pleasure-ground" — a castle-cottage in the suburb of Walworth. Gothic buildings sprang up all over London in Dickens' time — although one with a moat, drawbridge and rooftop cannon was more unusual.

E.T. Archive

But Dickens is at pains to point out that life is not really like that. Pip discovers that Miss Havisham, far from being a good fairy-godmother, is really a tormented witch; that Estella is no beautiful princess but a flint-hearted temptress. Pip finally discovers that in order to 'live happily ever after' he must first undergo the painful process of finding out who he really is.

AN IDEAL GENTLEMAN
Pip's agonized rejection of Joe and all he stands for is at the centre of the novel. In his boyhood he thinks of him as "a larger species of child, and as no more than my equal". But when he sets about turning himself into a "London gentleman" his attitude changes; "how common Estella would consider Joe, a mere blacksmith; how thick his boots and how coarse his hands" and "If I could have kept him away by paying money, I would have paid money".

But Joe is also forgiving and unselfish and his heart is large. Joe represents a wider moral ideal of true 'gentlemanliness', expressed by Herbert Pocket's father.

"No man who was not a true gentleman at heart ever was, since the world began, a true gentleman in manner."

At the end of the book, Pip comes to realize that it is in the forge that the true gentleman is to be found. Far from being a "mere blacksmith", Joe Gargery is one of the heroes of the book, or as Dickens describes him "a gentle Christian man".

Convicts on the march
(left) More than 165,000 convicts were transported, crammed into overcrowded ships and herded like animals on arrival. Found guilty of any of 200 crimes, from petty theft to political nonconformism, they were assigned – virtually as slaves – as labour for the settlers.

Sandhurst, Victoria
(above) Gold mining towns attracted many ex-convicts. Some worked as bullock drivers, providing the only transport. Others became Squatters – illegal tenants – forming a new social class. A few made fortunes, in sheep or gold, although many starved or were killed.

CHARACTERS IN FOCUS

From the very first line of *Great Expectations*, vivid characters leap from the page. All have larger-than-life mannerisms, flaws and qualities typical of Dickens at his best.

Sensitive young Pip, the fearsome Magwitch and the eerie figure of Miss Havisham jostle with gentlemanly Herbert, Wemmick with his double life and a host of comic characters. Every human foible is represented – and a range of passions.

WHO'S WHO

Pip (Philip Pirrip) Hero and narrator. A sensitive orphan raised by his harsh sister in rural Kent. After mysteriously inheriting a fortune, he rejects his roots and moves to London to become a 'gentleman'.

Mrs Joe Gargery Pip's older sister. Bitter and niggardly, she raises Pip "by hand"–"a hard and heavy hand".

Joe Gargery Her long-suffering husband. A simple village blacksmith and gentle giant – and Pip's loyal friend and ally.

Miss Havisham A rich, eccentric lady, jilted on her wedding day many years before. Twisted by hatred and resentment, she lives in cobwebbed darkness.

Estella Her beautiful adopted daughter. Haughty and contemptuous, she has been brought up to wreak revenge on the male sex – on Miss Havisham's behalf.

Magwitch (alias Provis) A desperate convict. After terrifying young Pip into helping him, he is recaptured and transported, only to return–with dire results.

Jaggers A criminal lawyer in London. An awesome and unfeeling man, he is continually "washing his hands" of his underworld clients.

Wemmick Jaggers' confidential clerk. A dual personality – open and friendly at home in the country, stern and officious at work in London.

Herbert Pocket Pip's best friend. Kind, elegant and artlessly optimistic, yet living in genteel poverty, he proves to be an example of a true gentleman.

The fearsome lawyer Jaggers, both the terror and the only hope of half London's underworld, is "a burly man" with "bushy black eyebrows that . . . stood up bristling". He conducts conversations like cross-examinations, characteristically throwing his large forefinger at the 'defendant'.

The honest blacksmith was something of a Victorian rural ideal; Joe Gargery is presented as a simple soul, "awful dull" by his own account, and "common . . . a mere blacksmith" in the prejudiced view of young Pip. Yet Joe is Pip's most constant ally, and with his "strong hand . . . quiet tongue and . . . gentle heart" is an example of a gentleman. He is a "gentle Christian man".

Mary Evans Picture Library

"The strangest lady I have ever seen. . ." is Pip's first impression of Miss Havisham – "a waxwork and skeleton that moved and looked at me". She is both awesome and frightening to his child's eyes. Her half-life in a world of decayed and decaying grandeur, where "speckled-legged spiders with blotchy bodies" run in and out of her putrid wedding feast, both repels and attracts him, creating aspirations beyond his own simple background and false ideas of 'gentlemanliness'.

Mary Evans Picture Library

W.P. Frith: The Railway Station (detail/Bridgeman Art Library)

Pip, "the small bundle of shivers"
at the outset of the novel, soon grows into a
discontended, restless country lad who travels to
London to learn the arts of a gentleman. His child's
view of the world is both comical and acute but
leads the adult Pip into brutally honest admissions.
"But I never thought there was anything low and
small in my keeping away from Joe . . ." he says
as he abandons his childhood companion. Pip's
friend Herbert Pocket has, by contrast, "a natural
incapacity to do anything secret or mean".
Herbert's good humour and open nature survive
material poverty and he becomes a shining
example of what a true gentleman should be and
how a true gentleman should behave.

The ridiculous Mr Wopsle is a marvellous
comic creation. His hopeless pursuit of fame
also underlines one of the main themes of
the book: that pride comes before a fall.
Pip's rejection of his own background
as he strives to become a gentleman
is paralleled by Wopsle abandoning
the Church – and his name – to
become an actor. His trumpeted
career is a pathetic and
laughable sham, and
both he and Pip appear
ridiculous for choosing
appearance rather
than reality.

Bridgeman Art Library

"Very proud . . . very pretty . . . very insulting", Estella instantly
captures Pip's heart. This portrait – *La Coranto* by William Frith – epitomizes
the Victorian ideal on which Estella is modelled. When Miss Havisham
accuses her of being a "stock and stone", a "cold, cold heart", Estella replies,
" 'I am what you have made me.' " She is not only the incarnation of Miss
Havisham's hatred in a young and beautiful form, she is also the embodiment
of gentility without gentleness – the very opposite of Joe. Impressionable Pip
is quite unconvinced by her assertion that "I have no heart . . . no – sympathy
– sentiment – nonsense" and loves her – at the cost of his peace of mind.

CRUSADER FOR LIFE

He was 'the National Sparkler', lightening the drab lives of his readers. But he also waged war against the darkness of injustice with all the heat of a firebrand.

'As to my art,' wrote Charles Dickens in 1860, 'I have as great a delight in it as the most enthusiastic of my readers.' During the second half of his writing life, he continued to perform as 'the National Sparkler' – a copious, energetic and endlessly inventive entertainer. But Dickens never stood still, as a man or as a writer. And from the 1850s he evolved a more carefully wrought structure and style, his characters became psychologically more complex, and his vision of the world grew perceptibly darker and more menacing.

This last development showed itself in Dickens' more pessimistic attitude towards British society. He remained a reformer, passionately denouncing the evils of the age, but his later fiction is less concerned with specific abuses than with larger, often seemingly incurable ills. In novels such as *Bleak House* and *Little Dorrit*, lives are not destroyed by a particular bad law, but by 'the majesty of the Law' itself – which is in turn only the corrupt instrument of a society corrupt from top to bottom.

SYMBOLS OF EVIL

In several of Dickens' later novels the darker mood is conveyed through the highly effective use of recurrent symbolic images. In *Bleak House*, town and country are swathed in a thick, blinding, stifling fog – a meteorological equivalent to the Court of Chancery. *Little Dorrit*, a novel whose characters dwell in actual or mental prisons, is dominated by the Marshalsea gaol. And in *Our Mutual Friend*, the hideous mountains of refuse that threaten to overwhelm London are the chief source of wealth in the book, where muck and money both pollute; this image was something of a favourite with Dickens, who elsewhere referred scornfully to Parliament as 'the Great Dust Heap down at Westminster'.

In *Bleak House*, Dickens focuses his attack upon the Court of Chancery, where the seemingly never-ending law suit of Jarndyce and Jarndyce – which is dealing with a dispute over the distribution of an estate – is finally resolved only when the cost of the suit has absorbed all money in the estate. Meanwhile, the lives of those involved have been devastated. This attack hit home: at a Mansion House dinner, where Dickens was present, the Vice-Chancellor made a speech in which he felt obliged to blame any tardiness in the legal system on the miserliness of the public who had only just agreed to an increase in the number of judges. While speaking, the Vice-Chancellor looked pointedly at Dickens out of all the guests.

Bleak House does not confine its attacks to the legal system. Dickens uses the bitterest irony and the harshest satire to expose the hypocrisy and self-interest embodied both in institutions (such as the

J. C. Horsey: The Crossing Sweeper/Cider House Galleries Ltd/Bridgeman

G. Durand: Lambeth Market/Christopher Wood Gallery, London/Bridgeman

'Phiz'
Hablot Knight Browne (right), who signed himself 'Phiz', was Dickens' favourite illustrator. He was capable of including vital detail – such as the "towsling" of Annie Strong (far right) whose seduction could only be hinted at in the text of David Copperfield.

Varied humanity
Dickens' writings appealed to a far bigger public than usually read or bought books. He created characters of every social station (left), drawing not only on personal experience but on an instinctive understanding of the bustling humanity for whom he wrote (below).

aristocratic party government of "Coodle and Boodle") and individuals. There are the 'do-gooders' Mrs Pardiggle and Mrs Jellyby, who are so absorbed in self-righteous acts of Charity that they are blind to the suffering immediately around them. The itinerant preacher Mr Chadband substitutes sonorous but meaningless oratory for a genuinely Christian attitude. And "Chancellor" Krook, the rag-and-bone-man parody of the real Lord Chancellor, is, in his greed and useless accumulation of piles of legal papers (which he cannot read), an obvious comment on the over-blown, self-perpetuating bureaucracy of the Court of Chancery.

Krook's existence underlines the fact that corrupt self-interest is in evidence from the 'top' to the 'bottom' of the land. And through the various complex but interconnected threads of the story, Dickens shows how those with privilege, power and money either ignore or exploit the poor and powerless – symbolized particularly by Jo the orphaned crossing sweeper, who lives and dies in disease-ridden squalor.

HEART VERSUS HEAD
While *Bleak House* addresses a vast social panorama, Dickens' next novel, *Hard Times*, is both shorter in length and more concise in its condemnation. In it, Dickens turned the full battery of his art on the inhumanity and soullessness of Victorian materialism. Set in a mill town in the 1840s, when industrial expansion was at its height, it shows with awful clarity the

Philanthropic friend
Baroness Burdett-Coutts (right) joined forces with Dickens the reformer, but took fright at what she saw as his dangerous radicalism.

dehumanizing results of capitalist 'Utilitarian' ethics, which insisted on the primary importance of high profits (and, therefore, cheap labour) for the good of the country. Part of this ethic was the worship of quantifiable facts and observably 'useful' behaviour – love, imagination and creativity have no place. In this world, human beings are reduced to numbers in the industrial machine.

Dickens' despair at the condition of

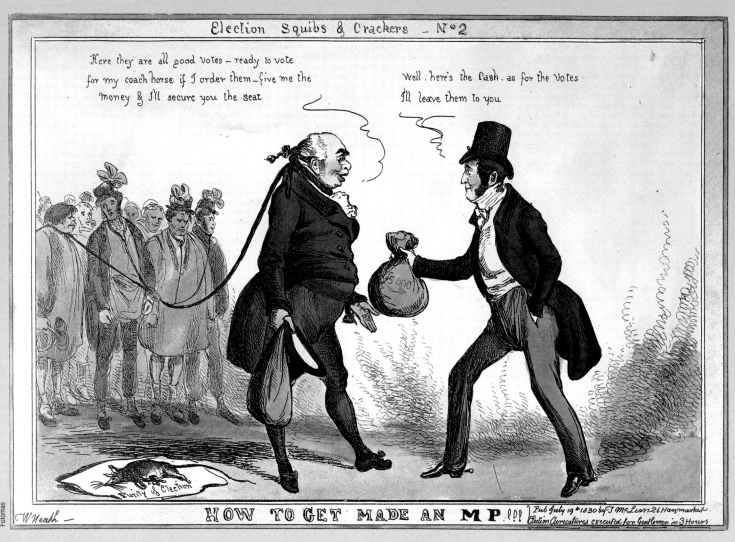

HOW TO GET MADE AN MP !!!

Corruption in high places

Electoral rigging (above) was one of the evils to which Dickens addressed himself. In the absence of an effective democratic process, his role as 'voice of the Poor' was all-important.

Writing to the end

Dickens' energy never flagged, and late in life he continued to pour out fiction and non-fiction in spite of declining health.

English society was at its deepest during the years that he was writing *Hard Times*, and his next novel *Little Dorrit*. The end of the Crimean War in 1856 – which had been an excuse for Parliament not to proceed with reforms at home – was greeted with apathy, and Dickens became increasingly sceptical that real social change could or would come about through the conventional channels. At times he even doubted the public's own strength of will, and wrote 'I know of nothing that can be done beyond keeping their wrongs continually before them.'

He kept their wrongs before them in his articles and in *Little Dorrit*, in which every character is tainted to some extent with the vices of greed and self-interest that permeate society. Not everyone liked having their 'universal' faults pointed out: one exasperated reviewer of *Little Dorrit* demanded 'Who is this man who is so much wiser than the rest of the world that he can pour contempt on all the institutions of his country?'

TIRELESS CAMPAIGNER

Until the end of his life, Dickens worked as hard as ever to change the world, both in novels and in crusading articles in *Household Words* and *All the Year Round*. He continued to demand government action to promote mass education, government regulation of industry to bring down the horrifyingly large numbers of industrial accidents, 'houses, instead of polluted dens' for the working class, and a range of related reforms.

Poor health and increasingly complex intentions made creative work more difficult as Dickens grew older. By 1864 he was noting that 'I have grown hard to satisfy, and write very slowly.' His professionalism never deserted him, however, and when the circulation of his magazines needed to be lifted, he would set himself to write a novel in brief weekly parts – a requirement that accounts for the unusually compact form and treatment of *Hard Times* and *A Tale of Two Cities*. Although his colours became more sombre, he always gave his readers a full measure of narrative thrills and comic absurdities which carried them with him to the very end of the story.

And Dickens' political sympathies remained fundamentally unaltered. In the last year of his life he declared that he had 'very little faith in the people who govern us' but 'great confidence in the People whom they govern'. At his death, Dickens was not only the most illustrious writer of his time, he was also still performing his dual roles, as 'the Inimitable' or 'National Sparkler' and as the uncompromising keeper of the Victorian conscience.

During the second half of his life, Dickens' vision darkened, though he remained hugely energetic and inventive. In *David Copperfield* (1850), the most autobiographical of his books, he drew heavily on memories of his youth. *Bleak House* (1853) was the first of his novels to use an all-pervading symbol – fog, which, like the Law, muddled and blinded everyone caught up in it. In *Hard Times* (1854) he hit out against the callousness of industrial masters, while *Little Dorrit* (1857) deals with London's dubious financiers and debtors' prison. After a thrilling excursion into history with *A Tale of Two Cities* (1859), Dickens exposed the corrupting influence of genteel pretensions in *Great Expectations* (1861). *Our Mutual Friend* (1865), with its images of filth and murder for love and money, is Dickens' darkest book. The unfinished *The Mystery of Edwin Drood* (1870) saw a new style emerging which, tragically, he did not live to develop. All this while, he was still intensely active as an editor, publisher and journalist.

DAVID COPPERFIELD

◆ 1850 ◆

This is the "autobiography" of David (right), whose early years are spent with his pretty, weak mother and faithful servant Clara Peggotty. A happy holiday is spent in Great Yarmouth with Clara's relations, including the delightful Little Emily. But on his return, David finds his mother has married Edward Murdstone, a coldly self-righteous tyrant. Sent away to a harsh school, David is befriended by the charismatic James Steerforth, but when his mother dies, he is wholly at the mercy of his step-father. A long, arduous climb faces him, and those who befriend, exploit, love and threaten him include some of Dickens' most famous characters: Betsy Trotwood who hates donkeys, the "'umble" clerk Uriah Heep, the helplessly pretty Dora Spenlow, Barkis the carrier, Tommy Traddles and the impecunious Mr Micawber (below).

Christopher Wood Gallery, London/Bridgeman

BLEAK HOUSE

◆ 1853 ◆

In the court of Chancery (right), the case of Jarndyce versus Jarndyce drags on and the slow workings of the Law blight many, many lives. Esther Summerson, an orphan adopted by the kind John Jarndyce, becomes housekeeper at his home, Bleak House, and companion to his wards, Richard Carstone and Ada Clare, who are in love. The Chancery case has heart-rending consequences for them all.

Meanwhile, a mysterious connection comes gradually to light between Esther and the frozen-hearted Lady Dedlock which intrigues the lawyer Tulkinghorn. He sets out to investigate but, after finding the body of one poisoned man, Nemo (whose name means No-one), the inquisitive Tulkinghorn is murdered.

Suspicion falls on Lady Dedlock, and when her secrets are laid bare it becomes plain that her cold-heartedness conceals an all-too-passionate past. Vindication comes too late to save her life.

Dickens derived some of his hatred of the legal system from his own frustrating and unprofitable efforts to sue pirate publishers. He perceived that the only victors in any legal wrangle are the lawyers, assured of their fat fee whichever side they represent.

Guildhall, London/Bridgeman Art Library

HARD TIMES

◆ 1854 ◆

Illustrated London News Picture Library

The dark, satanic mills of the industrial North (left) are the setting for this, the shortest of Dickens' novels. Thomas Gradgrind, a retired merchant of "Coketown", believes that life and the world should be governed by Fact. He is contemptuous of imagination and emotion, and thanks to the upbringing he has given them, Gradgrind's children, Louisa and Tom, are inadequate human beings.

Louisa marries the much older Josiah Bounderby, a bragging, self-made man. The feckless Tom robs Bounderby's bank. However, suspicion falls on the unhappy Stephen Blackpool, unpopular because of his independence of mind and unhappy because he is tied by law to a drunken wife.

Louisa, disillusioned with her marriage, does not discourage the attentions of well-bred, if languid, James Harthouse, but when matters come to a head, where else can she flee but to the unlikely protection of her dour father?

Guilt, accusations, recriminations and punishment fall thick and fast and Gradgrind is forced to reassess the values on which he has shaped his and his children's lives.

The novel is a harsh indictment of both the industrial practices and the philosophical outlooks of Victorian England. Though some greeted its serialized publication in *Household Words* with conservative unease at its radical sentiments, it quickly doubled the magazine's circulation. By the time the serial ended, *Household Words* was five times more profitable.

City of York Art Gallery, York/Bridgeman

OUR MUTUAL FRIEND

→ 1865 ←

Gaffer Hexam makes a living retrieving corpses from the Thames (below). Deeply ashamed of his trade, his daughter Lizzie allows it to blight her chances of marriage to the man she loves. One night Hexam pulls from the river a body bearing the identification of John Harmon, heir to the fortune of a "dust-collector". The fortune at stake has been amassed from the mountains of filth in London's streets – the book treats money as synonymous with dirt and corruption.

John Harmon is not dead. He has exchanged clothes and identities with a sailor. Calling himself John Rokesmith, he becomes the secretary of Noddy Boffin who has given Bella Wilfer a home. "Rokesmith" falls in love with her, but she is set on marrying money. Events, however, cause her to reassess her attitudes.

The love stories of Lizzie Hexam and Bella Wilfer run parallel, as love struggles in both cases to outshine the darkness of filthy lucre.

LITTLE DORRIT

→ 1857 ←

Amy (nicknamed "Little Dorrit") (above) supports her family single-handed by sewing for Mrs Clennam. Her complacent, selfish father, William Dorrit, has found himself a comfortable niche in the Marshalsea debtors' prison. Mrs Clennam is strangely hostile towards her son Arthur, newly returned from the East. Attracted to Little Dorrit, Arthur tries to help her father, but his efforts are foiled.

Then William Dorrit inherits a fortune and leaves prison, but dies abroad, so that Amy is now rich. Arthur is ruined by the death of a defaulting banker and in turn finds himself in the Marshalsea. Little Dorrit is prepared to sacrifice her entire fortune to help him, but Arthur will not hear of it.

Blackmail, illegitimacy and villainy raise their heads in this story overshadowed by the grim turrets of the debtors' prison – a place Dickens knew all too well from his youth.

The Museum of London

THE MYSTERY OF EDWIN DROOD

→ 1870 ←

Declarations of love, both welcome and unwelcome, besiege Rosa Bud (left) in this dark tale of suspected murder. The novel is set in a cathedral town where John Jasper is choir-master. Despite his outward respectability, he is an opium addict and a man of strong, repressed passions. His ward, Edwin Drood, has been pledged since childhood to Rosa Bud, though the enforced tie seems to render love impossible between them. Neville Landless is a fiercely jealous and aggressive rival to Edwin and, when Edwin disappears, suspicion of murder readily falls on him. But when Jasper declares his love for Rosa, the reader becomes increasingly convinced that it is he who has done away with his ward. Meanwhile a stranger, Dick Datchery, is investigating the mystery . . . No-one knows how Dickens intended his half-completed novel to end.

Dickens' London

The noisy, bustling, crowded streets of 19th-century London — to which Dickens felt the 'attraction of repulsion' — were at the heart of his world and a constant source of inspiration.

The London of Dickens' imagination, the London recreated and described in his major novels, is essentially the London of the 1820s – the scene of his childhood and early manhood. It is the portrait of a city not yet hidden under the smog of Victorian prudery – a city brimming with life.

Already the largest city in Europe when Dickens was born in 1812, London was to become the first city in the world by the time of his death. Into this melting-pot poured the rural poor of England and poverty-stricken Ireland, in search of plentiful work building London's railways and the great institutions of the wealthy Empire.

AN EXPLODING POPULATION

Increasing from one to three million in Dickens' lifetime, London's population spread out from the centre, northwards – to Hampstead, Highgate and Kentish Town – and southwards to Clapham, Brixton, Wandsworth and Walworth ("a collection of back lanes, ditches, and little gardens" where Wemmick in *Great Expectations* keeps an eccentric household). Only a generation earlier – the time of the French Revolution – sheep had grazed in Soho Square, and open fields bordered north Oxford Street.

But Dickens' London was essentially the subterranean world of the poor. Huddled together in what came to be known as 'Rookeries' – the poor banded together in large numbers, like rooks – the vast class of London's down-and-outs scratched a living. It was a world of vice and squalor that few of London's respectable classes even knew existed – places like Jacob's Island, a rotting, reeking, rabbit-warren of courtyards and alleyways in Bermondsey where barefoot and half-naked infants splashed about in excrement and slime. It is the London seen by the ragged orphan Oliver Twist.

The ways were foul and narrow; the shops and houses wretched; and people half-naked, drunken, slipshod and ugly. Alleys and arches, like so many cesspools, disgorged their offences of smell and dirt, and life upon the streets; and the whole quarter reeked with crime, and filth and misery.

And festering in the heart of London was the most notorious 'Rookery' of all, Seven Dials – the area at the top of St Martin's, close to Covent Garden – where Dickens witnessed 'wild visions of wickedness, want and beggary'. Here over 3,000 people were packed into fewer than a hundred houses. When on one occasion a house caught fire, 37 men, women and children were found occupying a single room – with just one shilling between them all. It was conditions like these, as Dickens recognized, that provided an ideal breeding ground for crime and prostitution.

Not surprisingly in a city overpopulated and poorly housed, disease was rife. Infant mortality was common – a fact noted in many of Dickens' novels – and the city suffered from periodic epidemics of typhus, cholera and smallpox. The major cause of disease was bad drainage and inadequate sanitation. Between Putney

Alfred Dunhill Collection/E.T. Archive

Public executions
(right) The 'wickedness and levity' of the crowds gathering at these events appalled Dickens. Street hangings were a common feature of London until 1869.

High society
(below) The elegance of Regent Street, built in Dickens' youth, testified to the wealth of the largest city in the world. Running north from Piccadilly Circus, Regent Street was one of the thoroughfares separating fashionable London from the more squalid suburbs.

Mansell Collection

E.T. Archive

and Blackwall, 369 sewers discharged their effluent into the River Thames, together with waste from tar and tanning factories and slaughterhouses.

Yet at low tide, the scummy mud banks of the pestilent Thames provided a 'living' of sorts for one of the many species of scavengers infesting London – the so-called 'Mudlarks', mainly young children who sifted the sewer exits for saleable items, or stole pieces of coal from barges.

THE UNDERWORLD

The 'low girls' who plied their trade at Seven Dials were just a few of the vast army of prostitutes that walked the streets of London in Dickens' time. Writing in 1851, Dickens' contemporary, Henry Mayhew, in his *London Labour and London Poor,* calculated that there were some 80,000 'board lodgers', 'sailors' women', or 'dolly mops' (some barely in their teens) in London alone. These women were not confined to the poorer parts, either. The greatest number was to be found in 'the brilliant gaiety of Regent Street and the Haymarket' where streetwalkers catered for all pockets and tastes, while private establishments conducted their business in a more leisurely manner.

While Dickens avoided any specific portrayal of prostitutes in his writing, their plight – caught as they were in a web of poverty, destitution and disease – prompted him to act. In 1846 he helped the wealthy philanthropist Angela Burdett Coutts to establish a home for fallen women (known as Urania Cottage) in Shepherd's Bush. Dickens had few illusions about what could be done, but he hoped that care, sympathy and understanding would encourage them to start a new life in Australia or to marry and settle down.

Prostitution was by no means the only social problem endemic in the poorer parts of the city. Thieves, burglars, forgers, card-sharps and con-men abounded. Mayhew did not even attempt to number them, though Dickens was to chronicle their activities and describe their haunts in his radical journalism of the 1850s and in short pieces such as *A Night Scene in London* (1856). There were, according to police estimates, some 3,000 houses of 'bad character' which were likely to receive stolen goods. The 'Rookeries' served as refuges for many gangs (such as that run by the malevolent Fagin in *Oliver Twist*), who could elude pursuit in the sunless labyrinths and enjoy the hospitality of 'flash houses' – establishments that combined the appeal of the public house and the brothel as well as providing exits for customers on the run.

In Dickens' youth, the 'Robin Redbreasts', red-waistcoated Bow Street runners, failed to stem the London crime wave. However, matters improved somewhat with the introduction, in 1829, of 'bobbies' or 'peelers' (so-called after the Home Secretary of the day, Sir Robert Peel).

Those who fell into the arms of the law received little mercy – harsh retribution was the stock-in-trade of a perverse, tyrannical and unforgiving legal system. Jaggers' character and the nature of 'Little Britain' in *Great Expectations* was no exaggeration. Britain's prisons were among the worst in Europe, and London's Newgate (to which Dickens was a frequent visitor) was one of the worst in Britain. These centres of human

On the streets
(above) 'Costermongers', street traders, pick-pocket and child crossing-sweepers were all part of the shifting population of London's changing streets.

'The Rookeries'
(left) Wild Court, Seven Dials – where up to 40 people occupied a single room, and Dickens witnessed 'wild visions of wickedness'.

Waifs and strays
(below) Pathetic, destitute, abandoned children were, Dickens said, 'one of the worst sights in London'.

degradation were specifically designed to deter the would-be criminal and were made so appalling that no-one could tolerate a return visit. It was a policy that Dickens, surprisingly, endorsed – though he did campaign vigorously against capital punishment and the popular public hangings, then a feature of London life. When George Manning and his wife were 'topped' at Horsemonger Lane in 1849, Dickens was just one of 30,000 Londoners who witnessed the scene. 'The conduct of the people', he wrote in a letter to *The Times,* 'was so indescribably frightful, that I felt for some time afterwards almost as if I were living in a city of devils.'

"AN AMAZING PLACE"

The Londoners who people the pages of Dickens' fiction – from Sam Weller, the cheerful cockney in *The Pickwick Papers* (1837), to John Jasper, who visits the opium dens of the Docklands in *The Mystery of Edwin Drood* (1870) – were observed by Dickens at first hand on his energetic walks through the city. He would think nothing of covering eight to ten miles a night, northwards to Highgate or westwards to Fulham, to clear his mind after a day's writing and to gather fresh impressions which were later woven into his novels.

Life in all its shapes and forms crowded the noisy, bustling, streets of London. Some 30,000 'costermongers' engaged in the sale of fruit, vegetables, and fish. Notoriously a turbulent tribe, politically radical, and sworn enemies of the police, they kept themselves to themselves, separate even from other street folk.

Jostling with the 'costers' for custom were traders and hawkers selling their wares. Beggars were also a

The railway boom
(below) The railways changed the face of Dickens' London – thousands of homes were swept aside to make way for them.

common sight, and they would often fake afflictions to gain sympathy – and a few pennies.

London, as David Copperfield observed, was "an amazing place", richer in wonderment "than all the cities of the earth". The sights that had delighted the young Dickens in his youth – the street entertainers, musicians, dancers, clowns and acrobats, as well as showmen with mini-theatres such as Punch and Judy and the marionettes of the Fantoccini Man – were still a feature of the Victorian City.

The noise that bombarded the pedestrian was deafening. Coaches, private carriages, hackney cabs, carts and wagons clattered through thoroughfares, many still narrow and winding. Congestion was frequent, and lack of regulation often led to chaos as omnibuses crossed from the left-hand side to the right, obligingly dropping passengers at their doorsteps.

London's entertainments
(left and below) Dickens loved the theatre – a passion shared by high-brow and low-life alike. With London's theatre, the two worlds could collide: young bloods would mingle with prostitutes and drunks in the coffee-houses close to the theatres, such as this one near the Olympic.

It was all, as Dickens said, like a marvellous magic lantern – a stimulus to his work that he found difficult to do without when abroad or even when staying in the country for any length of time. 'Put me down to Waterloo Bridge at eight o'clock in the evening,' he wrote to his friend John Forster from Italy, 'and I would come home . . . panting to go on. I am sadly strange as it is, and can't settle.'

CITY OF CHANGE

With success, Dickens left the back streets of Camden Town – where he had lived as a boy – far behind. After writing *Pickwick Papers* and *Oliver Twist* he moved first to 1 Devonshire Terrace, a splendid Nash building near to Regent's Park. In 1851 he moved to the larger Tavistock House in Tavistock Square, on the borders of Bloomsbury. But the life that he led here and in fashionable society – riding in the new hansom cabs, and shopping at Fortnum and Mason's – seems not to have stirred his imagination at all. It was the poorer, but more colourful, districts which repelled but also attracted him, to which he returned time and again for inspiration.

In the 58 years of Dickens' life, London underwent drastic changes. Many of London's landmarks were new, or of very recent vintage, when Dickens was young: Regent Street, Regent's Park with its spacious terraces, Buckingham Palace, the Haymarket, Trafalgar Square and Nelson's Column (erected in 1843) and the new House of Commons – built on the ashes of the old (where Dickens had been a reporter) in 1834.

Reforms and improvements urged upon a reluctant government by Dickens and other humanitarian reformers – slum clearance, decent sanitation, adequate street lighting and proper policing – had been carried out. There were still great stretches of slums, but some of the worst were knocked down to make way for

Covent Garden *(above) "when it was market morning was wonderful company." (*Uncommercial Traveller*).*

49

new thoroughfares – and the first 'model' housing developments were laid out. After the 'Great Stink' of 1858, when an exceptionally hot dry summer forced a mass evacuation from the Thames – and the Houses of Parliament – a new and effective main drainage system was devised. Respectable opinion finally put an end to public executions in 1869. The Victoria, Albert and Chelsea Embankments were constructed and more and more bridges spanned the Thames. The great London railway termini were built, and the new suburban lines and the Underground Railway (opened in 1863) advanced the revolution in communications.

Consequently, Dickens' Londoners lived in a world more exciting but also more precarious than their ancestors'. In the commercial and financial heart of the first-ever industrial nation, there were opportunities galore for the energetic or rich. But there were also new insecurities as booms and slumps alternately created business empires and bankruptcies, good wages followed by unemployment – reversals of fortune that play so large a part in Dickens' novels. Thousands lost their homes as those new thoroughfares and housing developments were laid out, and many more thousands were dispossessed when whole communities were destroyed to make way for London's railway system. Existence in London was taking on the rootless, anonymous quality now associated with big cities everywhere.

Dickens was the first novelist to chronicle the life of London. For millions of readers he charted a strange and unknown land full of mystery and terror. 'Life in London as revealed in the pages of Boz,' wrote Richard Ford of the influential *Quarterly Review,* 'opens a new world to thousands bred and born in the same city. . .for the one half of mankind lives without knowing how the other half dies'. And Dickens' popularity (his publishers Chapman and Hall sold 4,239,000 volumes in the first twelve years after his death) ensured that his view of the city became familiar to the whole nation. As his contemporary Walter Bagehot wrote, 'Dickens describes London like a special correspondent for posterity'.

Royal Holloway College/Bridgeman Art Library

Newgate prison
(above) The most notorious of London's prisons, Newgate both fascinated and revolted Dickens. In Great Expectations, *the "grim stone building" near Jaggers' office is one of Pip's first sights of the City. "This was horrible, and gave me a sickening idea of London."*

Sally Holmes

DICKENS' LONDON TODAY
1: 48 Doughty Street. Dickens' home from 1837–9 is now a museum.
2: Seven Dials. The dense labyrinth of slums was a focus of Dickens' interest in crime.
3: Adelphi Theatre. Dickens' love of the theatre inspired his public readings. The Adelphi is mentioned in *The Pickwick Papers.*
4: Lincoln's Inn. The heart of the English legal system in *Bleak House.*
5: St Dunstan's, Fleet Street. The church that inspired *The Chimes* also occurs in *David Copperfield.*
6: St Paul's Cathedral occurs in many of the novels.
7: The Guildhall houses the City Giants, Gog and Magog, in *Pickwick Papers.*
8: The George Inn. A galleried inn of the type visited by Mr Pickwick.

THOMAS HARDY

✦ *1840-1928* ✦

From humble beginnings in rural Dorset, Thomas Hardy rose to
achieve the social prominence he craved, but he remained torn
between the 'dream country' of his imagination and the world of
London's literati. His genius lay in portraying the pastoral life he
knew so well – but the honesty with which he wrote about the
relationships between men and women outraged Victorian
sensibilities. When his last novel was publicly burned in 1896, he
withdrew to the country, and devoted himself to poetry.

A Divided Nature

Hardy achieved an elevated social status worlds away from his humble Dorset origins – yet his writing constantly drew him back to the rustic scenes of his boyhood.

The world of Hardy's novels is the world he knew intimately as a child and youth – that of rural Dorset. No subsequent experience gained so strong a hold on his imagination, even though he was to become a figure of outstanding literary fame, and was fêted by London society.

Born on 2 June, 1840, in the small Dorset village of Higher Bockhampton, baby Thomas appeared to be dead at birth, and was almost ignored in the surgeon's concern for his mother. Fortunately, both mother and child survived, and Thomas grew into the fragile, sensitive son of doting parents.

His mother, Jemima, was a youthful, vigorous woman. To young Thomas, she was more of an older sister than a mother, and her vivid personality and ideas were a lasting influence on him.

Hardy's father was a handsome, easy-going man, a stone-mason by trade and a talented amateur musician. Hardy's earliest memory was of being given a small accordian on his fourth birthday, and even at this age he loved to dance to the country tunes his father played. Hardy soon became adept at playing the fiddle himself, and – like his father – was much in demand at country dances and weddings.

At eight, Hardy went to the village school, which was run by the lady of the manor, Mrs Julia Martin. Their unusual fondness for each other probably gave rise to a recurrent theme in Hardy's earlier novels – that of love across class barriers. Years later she still

Ed Buziak

'a pink-faced youth'
(left) So Hardy described himself in his early twenties, when his innocent appearance reflected his sheltered upbringing.

Hardy's parents
(right) Thomas and Jemima shaped their son's future. From his father young Thomas inherited a talent for music and a love of Nature, while his mother remained a figure of the utmost importance throughout his life. Lively, intelligent and forceful, she was determined her son should be well educated – an ambition he was happy to share.

Architect's apprentice

(above) At the age of 16, Hardy began work for a Dorchester architect. These are his own drawings of capitals in Stinsford Church dating from this time. Hardy found his fellow pupil, Henry Bastow, lively and congenial, and spent much time joking, arguing and reading with him. He also began learning Greek, getting up at dawn to study by his bedroom window, before his walk in to work.

An idyllic birthplace
(left) Hardy was born in this isolated thatched cottage, which had been in the family since his grandfather built it in 1800. His early years were thus spent in the heart of the Dorset countryside, close to the sights, sounds and creatures of nature. He later recalled how in his childhood, he decided he did not want to grow up, or 'to be a man, or to possess things, but to remain as he was, in the same spot'.

called him 'dear little Tommy', while he described his relationship with her as 'almost that of a lover'. Perhaps because of maternal jealousy, Jemima Hardy removed her son from Mrs Martin's school the following year and took him to visit her sister in Hertfordshire.

Hardy's mother was determined he should be well-educated. She encouraged him to read widely and sent him to school in Dorchester where he learned Latin, French and German. Under her watchful eye, Hardy grew into an adolescent who, on his own account, was 'mentally precocious' but with a 'lateness of development in virility'. Despite, or perhaps because of, this he was emotionally susceptible from an early age.

In 1856, when Hardy was 16, he was articled to John Hicks, a Dorchester architect. It was here that Hardy met his close friend and mentor, the scholar and reviewer Horace Moule. Moule was eight years older than Hardy and had been educated at Cambridge. He was a charming and gentle man as well as a brilliant teacher. Together Moule and Hardy studied Greek drama and Moule encouraged his pupil to write poetry.

Also at this time, Hardy's morbid curiosity led him to witness several hangings – a common sight in the Assize town of Dorchester. The most memorable to Hardy was that of Martha Brown, who killed her husband in a crime of passion. Hardy never forgot 'how the tight black silk gown set off her shape as she wheeled half round and back'. Emotionally and factually, this memory inspired *Tess of the D'Urbervilles*.

In 1862 Hardy moved to London to pursue his career. Here he found work with Arthur Blomfield, specializing in church architecture. The boyish Hardy thus encountered for the first time the sophistication of city life. He also threw himself whole-heartedly into self-education, frequently visiting the theatre, opera and art galleries, and reading voraciously. Meanwhile an article he had written to amuse Arthur Blomfield's pupils – *How I Built Myself a House* – was published, and he began writing poems and submitting them to magazines, although none was accepted.

NEW ATTRACTIONS
On his 25th birthday, Hardy wrote: 'Feel as if I had lived a long time and done very little. Wondered what woman, if any, I should be thinking about in five years' time'. Such thoughts arose from his involvement with two of his cousins, who bore a strong resemblance to his mother – as did their youngest sister.

Hardy's next sweetheart was to be this cousin. Her name was Tryphena Sparks. Striking, dark-haired and independent, Tryphena was a teacher but was quickly promoted to become a headmistress in her twenties. Hardy spent an idyllic summer with her in 1869, but their divergent careers were destined to separate them. Always reticent about personal matters, Hardy's anguish found vent in his poetry, and in *Desperate Remedies*, the novel he was writing at the time. But Tryphena was to remain a type of perfection for him.

The following year, Hardy was sent to St Juliot in Cornwall, to supervise the restoration of the church. Here he met Emma Lavinia Gifford, the rector's sister-in-law. Emma was an energetic and adventurous woman, whose own literary ambitions enabled her to share keenly in the private world of his writing. Hardy's attraction was sharpened by her superior class (she was the daughter of a rich country solicitor). He described their first meeting as 'magic' – taking

Teacher and mentor
(above) The brilliant Horace Moule (seen here against the centre window), was Hardy's most influential friend in his early Dorchester days. Moule was an inspiration to Hardy, but was never able to realize his own potential.

Key Dates

1840 born in Higher Bockhampton, Dorset

1856–62 apprenticed to John Hicks, architect. Meets Horace Moule

1862 continues apprenticeship in London

1867 becomes involved with Tryphena Sparks

1870 meets Emma Gifford

1871 first novel, *Desperate Remedies*, published

1873 Moule commits suicide

1874 success of *Far From The Madding Crowd*. Marries Emma

1885 moves into Max Gate

1898 first book of poems published

1907 meets Florence Dugdale

1912 Emma dies. Florence becomes his secretary

1914 marries Florence

1928 dies in Dorset

place as it did against the glorious Cornish landscape.

Hardy's first literary success came with the serialization of *Far From The Madding Crowd* in 1874. Leslie Stephen, Thackeray's son-in-law, was the editor of the *Cornhill Magazine*, which published the story. He was the most influential man of letters in England at the time, and was to take the place of Horace Moule in Hardy's life.

While Hardy had been building a career, Moule had become enmeshed in his own personal tragedy. Incapable of making a success of his life, despite his intellectual gifts, he plunged into increasing bouts of depression, relieved only by drink. Sometimes he even slept with a razor under his pillow. Finally, in 1873, he committed suicide. His death profoundly affected Hardy's writing and darkened his view of fate.

MARRIED LIFE

Happier times were to follow for Hardy. Now established as a man of means, he married Emma Gifford on a lovely autumn day in 1874. None of Hardy's family was present and indeed he had taken pains to keep a distance between his fiancée and his relations. Even the manuscript of *Far From The Madding Crowd* was kept from Emma – it contained too much of his working-class background. Hardy's family were not to meet her for two years.

After several temporary addresses, the couple settled at Sturminster Newton. Hardy remembered their days here as 'Our happiest time'. Delighted with her newly-famous husband, Emma was anxious to please. She made copious notes and copies of quotations for Hardy's use in future novels, and their shared literary interests added a creative sparkle to their marriage. Their idyll did not last, however. Leslie Stephen's sister-in-law had told Hardy that an author should live in London; the couple moved to the city in 1878.

This move marked the beginning of a rift in the marriage. Silent and shy, Hardy was yet avid to observe and absorb the social scene. He loved the theatre – and the actresses – but would sit in his box hiding his face behind his hand, terrified of recognition. But while Thomas went to plays and parties, Emma stayed at home, growing fat and fretful. Nevertheless, she nursed him when he was prostrated for months by a bladder complaint.

Their life became divided between Dorset and London, with occasional visits to the Continent. This gratified Emma's love of Bohemianism, but the London visits also provided her husband ·with an increasing number of interesting female confidantes.

From about 1890 onwards, Emma was forced to concede victory to a series of society ladies, many of them strikingly attractive, intelligent women who

Life in Dorset
In 1885, Hardy and his wife Emma moved into Max Gate (left), the big redbrick house in Dorset he had designed himself. Hardy settled here permanently in old age, and was often to be seen cycling along the winding local lanes, but he frequented nearby Dorchester (below) very little.

The first Mrs Hardy
(left) Hardy married Emma Gifford after an idyllic, if interrupted, courtship. From their first meeting, Hardy was dazzled by Emma's sense of adventure and vitality. Her fearlessness complemented his own physical timidity, while he seemed to her the epitome of a glamorous London intellectual. She, too, was an aspiring writer, so the marriage seemed set fair for success. Sadly, however, their early years of happiness did not last. The more successful and sought-after Hardy became, the less he shared his life with Emma, until she lost what was perhaps dearest to her heart – their shared literary interests. Increasingly bitter and insecure, Emma began denigrating Hardy and his 'peasant origins', and kept a diary which she is said to have entitled 'What I think of my Husband'. Nevertheless, their early relationship was not only vindicated but immortalized after her death, when Hardy wrote some of his most moving and beautiful poems in memory of her.

epitomized the ideal which Hardy had first glimpsed in Tryphena Sparks. Most galling to Emma was that they often shared her literary ambitions – his associates included the poet Rosamund Tomson, with whom Hardy enjoyed the 'framing of rhymes', and Florence Henniker, a novelist and short-story writer.

These years were, nevertheless, the most successful for Hardy the writer. The publication of *Tess of the d'Urbervilles* finally assured his social status.

'THE END OF PROSE'

In 1892, Hardy's father died. With this further personal tragedy weighing him down, Hardy began work on what was to be his last, darkest and most controversial novel, *Jude the Obscure*.

The publication of the unexpurgated version in 1893 spelt the end of Hardy's novel-writing career, although it sold immensely well – 20,000 copies in the first three months. For Emma – who, again, had not seen the book in manuscript – it proved to be the last straw. Distressed by Hardy's continual neglect, Emma was now moved to fury. One of the main thrusts of the novel was a sustained attack on her deeply-held religious beliefs.

On 17th October, 1896, Hardy wrote that he had reached 'the end of prose'. This decision was only partly the result of the critical outcry at his last book. Hardy had suffered the first of many bouts of rheumatism and felt keenly the physical burden of writing long novels. This kind of writing also tended to become alarmingly self-revelatory. Hardy, a very private man, found personal memories and emotions crowding all too transparently on to the page. Poetry lent itself more readily to obscurity and ambiguity.

Though he had written poetry in almost every phase of his life, Hardy was at first uncertain whether his public would accept him as a poet. He need not have worried – his first published volume in 1898 was an immediate success. Indeed, it was as a poet that he was finally accepted as a scholar and a man of letters.

AN IDEAL WOMAN

Throughout his life, women were a continual and vital inspiration to Hardy. One of his earliest attachments was to his cousin, Tryphena Sparks, who resembled his mother in her dark and decided good looks and independent spirit. Her influence on Hardy continued long after the two had ceased to communicate. Her beauty and character are frequently echoed in Hardy's heroines – notably Sue Bridehead in *Jude the Obscure* – and in the type of society women for whom he often entertained wistful, adolescent infatuations. One of the most striking of these was Florence Henniker. Hardy adored her, calling her a "rare fair woman" in one of the numerous poems referring to her. Hardy often celebrated, or sublimated, his infatuations in poetry, and it says much for Florence's character that his passion was for once transformed into a genuine friendship.

From Outlines by Florence Henniker

Florence Henniker *– she survived his adoration to become a close friend.*

Tryphena Sparks *– Hardy's early love and an inspiration for his heroines.*

Hardy's main poetic work is a three-part verse epic, *The Dynasts*, set in the Napoleonic Wars. Between the publication of the first and second parts, his mother died. Much of what is known of his life and how such tragedies affected him is drawn from references and implications in the poems. It is, for example, a sad comment on his marriage that his first published volume includes love poems spanning 30 years of his life, of which only one is addressed to his wife.

Yet after Emma's death in 1912, she became for Hardy a "woman much missed", as the memories of their idyllic courtship came flooding back. In the following year, he wrote no fewer than 100 love poems to her – the most moving he ever wrote.

Hardy continued living at Max Gate, the gloomy house in Dorchester he had had built to his own design. The frugal, reclusive life he led earned him the dislike of the very people who had been so vital an inspiration for his novels. They considered him a snob, and children would chant 'Miser Hardy, miser Hardy' around the streets of Dorchester.

Hardy was further protected from the outside world by his second wife, Florence Dugdale. She began work for him as his secretary and they married in 1914. With her he wrote his autobiography, which was published

The hallmark of fame
(right) As an old man, Hardy no longer sought or needed society, but society continually demanded glimpses of him. Among the stream of visitors to Max Gate, his Dorset home, was perhaps the most socially distinguished of all. On 20 July 1923, Edward, Prince of Wales, drove through the streets of Dorchester with Hardy, before lunching at Max Gate with the writer.

Fact or Fiction

A MODEL FOR BATHSHEBA

Hardy's cousin, Tryphena Sparks, told him the unusual story of a local woman farmer. Catherine Hawkins had been widowed young, but despite her inexperience had resolved to run the family farm herself. During the terrible winter of 1865–66 she had been given invaluable help by a shepherd, whose sudden death left her in need. So began the creation of Bathsheba Everdene.

A spirited woman
(below) Hardy used a true story to construct Bathsheba's situation, but her strong character was suggested by that of his aunt who had emigrated with an ex-soldier.

Henry John Yeend King: By the Farm Gate/Fine Art Photographic Library

MERL, Reading/Dorset County Museum

A new wife
(left) Hardy met his second wife, Florence Dugdale, while he was still married to Emma. Like her, Florence considered herself a serious writer, and like Hardy she was Dorset-bred and from a working-class family. To Hardy, now 67, she brought back the "throbbings" of youth, and he typically rewarded her with a series of intense poems. What threatened to become an impossible situation was resolved by a Hardian stroke of fate. Emma died in 1912, and her role passed to Florence.

A last link with Oxford
(above) As a youth greedy for knowledge, Hardy – like his last hero, Jude – had dreamed of the spires of Oxford, which he saw as an ideal world of learning. The publication of his poetry at last brought Hardy unqualified success, and Oxford university was eager to recognize his importance by awarding him an honorary degree. This, together with honours from Cambridge, Aberdeen and St Andrew's, indicated Hardy's total acceptance by the English literary establishment.

after his death in his wife's name. In the process of writing it, they destroyed the personal papers on which it was based. This obsessive concern to conceal his lowly background led to a virtually fictional account of his early life.

Now firmly accepted by the English literary establishment, Hardy was more sought after than ever before. Visitors to Max Gate included Ramsay Macdonald, Virginia Woolf and Augustus John, a troupe of actors who performed *Tess* in the drawing room, American tourists and an Indian who had travelled 10,000 miles to speak to the great man, only to be denied access to him. Yet of those who were admitted, few were able to pierce the guard of Florence's vigilance and Hardy's mixture of silence and determined small talk. But remarkably, his poetry still flowed as effortlessly and beautifully as ever.

When he died on 11 January, 1928, the conflicting demands of nation and family dictated the somewhat unorthodox burial arrangements. His ashes were placed in Poets' Corner in Westminster Abbey, while his heart was buried in Stinsford Church in Dorset, with his first wife and his parents. The gulf between his humble origins and his exalted status remained with him even in death.

Love and Death

**Imaginative and compassionate in his writing, Hardy the man
was a strangely cold, complex individual who seemed able to
show love only to those he had lost through death.**

Lowly stock

*Hardy's father (below) was
a builder – a fact which
Thomas would like to have
concealed almost as much as
the fact that his mother was
pregnant at the time of his
parents' marriage. It is a sad
indictment of the novelist's
character that Thomas
Hardy senior was in fact a
sensitive, artistic man who
doted on his talented son.*

The picture of Hardy that emerges from the reminiscences of those who knew him is of a highly complex and contradictory personality. Edward Clodd, a friend of many years, in whom Hardy confided more than in most men, wrote that he 'was a great author: he was not a great man; there was no largeness of soul'. Yet 'largeness of soul' is the very quality critics and readers have particularly admired in Hardy's work. Was the man entirely separate from the writer – the one small, the other 'great'?

It is on record that Hardy was mean to his servants and that the children of Dorchester chanted 'Miser Hardy, miser Hardy' whenever he went by. Yet it is also a matter of fact that he generously undertook to look after his parents and two unmarried sisters (Mary and Kate) for most of their lives. Hardy also, it may be recalled, knew what it was to be poor. By nature he was frugal. His chosen profession offered little or no security, and he believed that a writer, if he was to maintain his integrity, should continue to live in the same style as before he achieved success.

Snobbery is another charge that has been levelled at Hardy, both during his lifetime and later. It is difficult to refute, since he deliberately created a false impression of his origins, education and the social standing of his parents, and neglected most of his relatives after having made his name as a writer. Perhaps most petty (and sad) was his wish to be known to be related, even though remotely, to the well-to-do. In *Who's Who* he provided the information that his wife (Emma) was the niece of an archdeacon. Such an entry is unique in that publication's history.

But snobbery is perhaps too harsh a judgement, for it neglects the deep division at the core of Hardy's life. Boldly stated, it amounted to this: to gain recognition as a writer – something he deeply craved – Hardy had to, or felt he had to, cut himself off from the very roots of his inspiration, the Dorset countryside and its

people. Yet, in order to write he had to live in Dorset, close to the scenes of his childhood – even though in almost every way, he no longer felt part of it.

Understandably, in one as hypersensitive as Hardy, this produced an almost intolerable tension. The theme of the 'return of the native' – of one who returns to his roots seeking his true self – is one to which Hardy turned again and again in his novels. This tension caused Hardy considerable unhappiness, but was his source of inspiration as a writer.

From an early age Hardy believed he was born to accomplish great things, and imbued his existence with an almost mythic significance. 'I never cared for Life', he wrote, 'Life cared for me'. Even his birth, he

Object of charity

*Hardy's mother, Jemima
(right), had at one time in
her life been dependent on
Poor Law charity. Despite
the extreme compassion
Hardy shows for the poor in
his novels, he was at pains to
'cover up' his humble origins
and went so far as to
perpetrate a mammoth
deception of the public in his
'Biography'.*

Loving cousins
Thomas (far left) and his cousin, Tryphena Sparks (left), may have been more than just friends when they spent time together in their youth. According to Tryphena's daughter, reminiscing more than 90 years later, her mother gave birth to an illegitimate son, Randal, who was Tryphena's and Thomas' lovechild. Although no birth certificate exists for the child, Tryphena did suddenly leave her post as headmistress of a school, aged 21, for no apparent reason, and a photograph of her with a baby boy in her arms has been found.

believed, was miraculous. To his last secretary, May O'Rourke, he claimed that he 'entered this world reluctantly, and so fraily that the surgeon attending laid him aside as already dead. Fortunately the nurse intervened and the infant was revived.'

LATE TO MANHOOD

As a boy, Hardy apparently knew that neither manhood nor possessions would bring him happiness. Was it a premonition of the difficult life to come? He probably thought so, for reviewing his life in old age he said that for him, growing up had been a slow and painful process. He was, he says, 'a child till . . . sixteen, a youth till . . . five-and-twenty, and a young man till . . . nearly fifty'.

That Hardy admitted this is in itself surprising, for he was, from an early age, the most reticent and secretive of men. When fame came to him in late middle-age he

went to extraordinary lengths to guard from public scrutiny not only his thoughts and feelings, but also the details of his origins and upbringing.

Today, the fact that Hardy was conceived out of wedlock, that his mother had been a recipient of Poor Law charity, that his father was a builder, and that among his close relations he numbered farm labourers and domestic servants, would do nothing to diminish his literary achievement – indeed quite the reverse. But at the time, Hardy felt that such personal details had to be hidden from the public at almost any cost. The means by which he attempted to do so involved him in one of the most curious deceptions in literary history.

Some months after his death in 1928, the first of his two-volume 'biography' was published, the concluding volume appearing two years afterwards. Although he maintained that the work was by his second wife, Florence, this claim fooled nobody; the work bore all the

A hard life
Hardy's birthplace (above left) influenced much of his writing. His friend the critic Edmund Gosse once asked, 'What has Providence done to Mr Hardy that he should rise up in the arable land of Wessex and shake his fist at his Creator?' For it was the harshness – as well as the beauty – of a life dependent on the elements which was an inspiration to Hardy.

Free-thinking friend
Edward Clodd (left) was a writer and banker living in Aldeburgh who gathered around him a group of men and women who, he felt, sympathized with his free-thinking beliefs. Hardy was one such, and they maintained a long-lasting friendship which foundered when, in old age, Hardy took up the practice of going to church. Clodd could not approve, nor could he find it in himself to praise Hardy after his death, except as a great writer.

hallmarks of Hardy's hand. And instead of killing biographical controversy, as he had intended, the deception, of course, fuelled interest in Hardy's life to an astonishing degree.

Hardy's life, particularly his early years, became the subject of intense speculation. His relationship with his cousin Tryphena Sparks has been seen by some to have involved more than mere cousinly friendship. Hardy, it has been claimed, fathered a child (called 'Randy') by Tryphena, but was prevented from marrying her by the revelation, made to him by his mother, that Tryphena was not his cousin, as he had supposed, but his niece. The resulting guilt and anguish he experienced, it is further claimed, accounts for the profoundly pessimistic view of life expressed in the novels.

Without endorsing this sensational and unsubstan-tiated claim, other biographers agree that Tryphena Sparks certainly had a profound effect on Hardy's life and that his not marrying her (for whatever reason) was the cause of much regret and unhappiness.

Hardy seems to have spent much of his life wishing things had been different. As an old man he expressed regret that he had not been a cathedral organist. He would, he said, rather have been that than anything else in the world. The past always seemed to Hardy to have been not only better than the present, but better than it seemed at the time.

RELIVING THE PAST

When Emma, his first wife, died after years of neglect and unhappiness, Hardy soon forgot their virtual estrangement from each other and remembered only their brief, idyllic courtship and first two years of marriage. It was a period of his life he was later to describe in a poem as "A preface without any book".

It is not easy to view Hardy's treatment of Emma with sympathy. It becomes even more difficult, knowing the sympathy he himself demanded of others. As a writer he showed great understanding in the creation of his characters, particularly his heroines. From Bathsheba Everdene in *Far From the Madding Crowd* to Tess in *Tess of the d'Urbervilles*, readers warmed to his sympathetic treatment of women. Yet, in life, Hardy acted with an insensitivity bordering on the callous.

Having neglected his first wife, Emma, in all but appearances during the last years of her life in favour of the much younger Florence Dugdale, Hardy proceeded to torture Florence after Emma's death, with vivid recollections in verse of the love he had once felt for Emma. For a woman even of Florence Dugdale's reputed saintly disposition, it must, on occasion, have been almost impossible to bear – particularly given Hardy's increasing lack of consideration towards her.

The first woman in Hardy's life, and the one who undoubtedly exerted the strongest influence over him, was his mother. She was bright and lively, and the two were almost dangerously attached to one another. The result was that the young Hardy grew up with the

Emma Lavinia Gifford
(above) Hardy's first wife was the daughter of a solicitor and niece of an eminent clergyman. As Hardy neglected her over the years, and idealized other women, Emma became convinced that she had married beneath her and that her own literary aspirations had been swamped by his. Yet, after her death, Hardy refers to Emma with the utmost tenderness, saying 'my life is intensely sad to me now without her'.

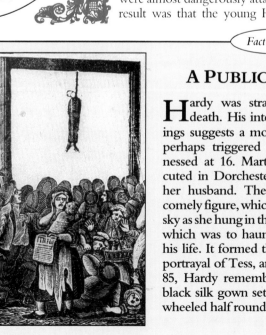

Fact or Fiction

A PUBLIC HANGING

Hardy was strangely fascinated by death. His interest in public hangings suggests a morbid frame of mind, perhaps triggered by a scene he witnessed at 16. Martha Brown was executed in Dorchester for the murder of her husband. The image of Martha's comely figure, which 'showed against the sky as she hung in the misty rain', was one which was to haunt Hardy throughout his life. It formed the inspiration for his portrayal of Tess, and, even at the age of 85, Hardy remembered 'how the tight black silk gown set off her shape as she wheeled half round and back'.

Moving with the times
Though backward-looking in his writing, Hardy was always first to welcome and adopt new inventions. At 82 he was a familiar sight on the streets of Dorchester, riding his safety cycle. The poet Molly Holden was even moved to write her eulogy 'TH' on seeing this particular photograph.

The younger woman
Florence Emily Dugdale, like Emma, was a writer who placed her talents at Hardy's disposal. She gave up a teaching job to become his secretary and assistant, and married him after Emma died. She was 35, he 39 years older – an old man haunted now by memories of his dead wife. For Florence married life proved to be 'lonely beyond words'. They are pictured (left) with their dog, Wessex.

image of an ideal woman who would be all to him that his mother had been, and more. The story of Hardy's romantic attachments is one of a lifelong search for such a woman, someone who could be both lover and mother to him, while allowing him to keep manhood at bay. What is surprising is that Hardy, with his intellect and understanding of human nature, never recognized that his search was doomed to failure.

Despite the impression created in the *Life* that he hardly spoke to a woman before the age of 30 – at which age he met his first wife, Emma Gifford – Hardy had, it seems, proposed not only to Tryphena but to her elder sisters, Martha and Rebecca.

A SEXUAL PORTRAIT

When, in his *Life*, Hardy admits to an inability to grow up, he attributes the cause to 'a lateness of development in virility' – hinting at some lack of sexual feeling, or of an inability to come to terms with his own sexuality. Sex, or what he called 'the strongest passion known to humanity', is certainly a major theme of the novels. Hardy seems to have explored his own sexuality and his own nature in a series of partial self-portraits in his fiction.

Like Henry Knight in *A Pair of Blue Eyes*, Hardy regarded himself as "not shaped by Nature for a marrying man". Clym Yeobright in *The Return of the Native*, like Hardy, is torn by the demands of a possessive mother and a passionately demanding wife. Angel Clare seeks through Tess his own lost purity, while Sue Bridehead in *Jude the Obscure* probably displays some of Hardy's own sexual inhibitions. All, like Hardy him-

A rare moment
Though once very sociable, Hardy in old age was withdrawn and reticent. His friend and biographer Rutland said, 'Hardy was not a man who in his maturity gave himself to others'. Gatherings like the one shown left (c. 1920) were rare.

'Most melancholy person'
A journalist wrote of Florence Hardy (below) that 'she smiled once but the smile only expressed sadness. She said she longed to go to America, "but I never shall," she said with a deep sigh, and with a still deeper sigh she said, "this place is too depressing for words in winter . . ."'

self, are idealists seeking through the loved one a return to a state of innocence, purity and joy, known only in childhood. As adults they seek, but are unable to find, happiness. In their search they enter into relationships which all end in disaster.

Significantly, the age at which Hardy says he finally reached maturity, 'fifty-six', was the age at which he completed his last novel, *Jude the Obscure*. From then on he wrote no more prose fiction, but turned instead to poetry. And in his poetry, if not in his life, Hardy was painstakingly honest about himself.

FLATTERY AND VANITY

Hardy moved further up the social ladder than perhaps any writer has ever done. While his origins were humble, honours and titles were showered on him in old age. Courted by society women, flattered by leading figures of his day, Hardy became almost an institution in his own lifetime. Yet behind the public face was a private man, deeply insecure.

Perhaps nowhere is this sense of insecurity shown more clearly than in his hypersensitive, almost paranoiac, reaction to the slightest criticism of his work. Though he hated reading about himself, he went through every article in which he featured with a fine-tooth comb, abusing the author for the slightest inaccuracy. Yet he steadfastly refused to discuss his work with anyone outside a small group of friends. In his relations with the critics, he was, in the estimation of E.M. Forster, 'very vain'.

This deep-seated insecurity resulted in what is perhaps one of the least attractive features of his life – his refusal to acknowledge the debt of gratitude he owed his first wife Emma for her devotion and encouragement of his early work, and for her considerable editorial help. In his defence it can only be said that Emma grew increasingly hostile towards Hardy, and hated his later books. She even tried to prevail on him to burn

REWRITING HISTORY

Realizing that he would be the subject of literary research after his death, Hardy, at 77, decided to write his own 'biography', *The Early Life of Thomas Hardy*, and pass it off as the work of his second wife, Florence. In the book he claims the term 'builder' meant his father supervised a substantial business, omits to mention that his mother was in service, and glosses over her need to marry. And his cousin, Tryphena Sparks, with whom he had an important early relationship, is not mentioned at all.

To ensure future biographers did not contradict him, he destroyed any letters, notebooks or diaries he thought too revealing. After his death, a gardener helped Florence burn more private papers in two great bonfires. 'It was a devil of a clearout,' he said.

This picture of Thomas Hardy at the age of 16 formed the frontispiece to his supposed biography.

From The Early Life of Thomas Hardy

Triumph without a smile

(below) Hardy fell ill and died in the winter of 1928. The tributes were many, the honours lavish. His hearse is pictured below leaving his home, Max Gate, for Woking where he was cremated. Beforehand he lay in state and his younger sister Kate said that he wore 'the same triumphant look' as the other corpses on view 'but without the smile'.

BBC Hulton Picture Library

his novel *Jude the Obscure* rather than allow it to be published.

Though he depended upon his wives totally, and demanded of them a respect bordering almost on adoration, Hardy gave little in return. Not once did he refer to Emma's intense suffering before her death. Indeed he wished the world to believe, and to believe himself, that her death had come both suddenly and unexpectedly.

In a draft of a poem, composed soon after her death, Hardy wrote of his wife's difficulty in climbing the stairs to bed and of that final *"calm evening when you climbed the stair,/ After a languid rising from your chair"*, with its hint of pain and impending sorrow. For publication, however, Hardy changed the lines to *"And that calm evening when you walked up the stair,/ After a gaiety prolonged and rare"*, thus removing all reference to her infirmity.

OLD AGE

Hardy was at the same time extremely preoccupied with his own health. While hypochondriac is perhaps too strong a term, Hardy took great interest in recording every change of mood and physical symptom suffered. 'I am in up and down spirits', he records in a letter to his friend Mrs Henniker in 1898. It is typical of the catalogue of complaints Mrs Henniker was bombarded with over the years – influenza, neuralgia, toothache, chills on the liver, headaches, loss of appetite are all noted. While still in his fifties, Hardy complains of feeling 'as weak as a cat' and of having 'no energy'. For a man so afflicted, it is a wonder he lived to the ripe old age of 87.

'Not a great man', but a 'great author' – his friend Edward Clodd's verdict seems inescapable. In a moment of self-revelation, Hardy wrote 'If way to the better there be, it exacts a full look at the worst'. Only as a poet did Hardy succeed in looking honestly at the worst in himself. And only as a writer did he succeed in revealing the best – his ability to understand, and movingly depict, the hardness of the human lot.

FAR FROM THE MADDING CROWD

**First of his 'dramas of country life and passions', this is the
masterpiece of Hardy's youth. His darkening vision had not yet cast
shadows over the sunny Wessex landscape.**

The story of *Far From The Madding Crowd* has much in common with the ballads that Hardy would have heard in his youth, with the faithful lover, the wicked and handsome soldier, the seduced maiden and the murder of a rival. But in Hardy's imagination, these simple 'folk' elements are transformed into the great themes of literature – love, suffering and betrayal – which reveal the 'eternal truth' about human relationships and humans' relationships with Nature. And it is in Hardy's evocation and celebration of English rural life that the novel achieves its unique appeal.

GUIDE TO THE PLOT

Far From The Madding Crowd is a story of a young woman-farmer and her three suitors. The faithful lover is Gabriel Oak, the honest young shepherd who is as reliable as his name implies. At 28 he is the master of a small but thriving sheep farm which he feels is enough to make him worthy of marrying the beguiling newcomer, Bathsheba Everdene.

The coquettish Bathsheba refuses Gabriel, who nevertheless professes a lifelong love for her and she shortly afterwards moves from Gabriel's village to manage Upper Farm at

> "*N*ow mind, you have a mistress instead of a master. I don't yet know my powers or my talents in farming; but I shall do my best, and if you serve me well, so shall I serve you.*"*

Weatherbury which she has inherited from her late uncle.

This rise in Bathsheba's fortune is mirrored by a severe fall in Gabriel's. He loses his sheep, his farm and all the wealth he had worked so hard to earn as a result of what Hardy described as a 'pastoral tragedy'. Forced to find employment elsewhere, the fallen farmer ends up being taken into Bathsheba's service as a shepherd.

On a neighbouring farm to Bathsheba's, lives the handsome but reserved Mr Boldwood. Boldwood is "the nearest approach to aristocracy that this remoter corner of the parish could boast of." Bathsheba first notices him in Casterbridge marketplace, only because he fails to notice her. Used to being admired by all around her, she is intrigued by his aloofness. As an impulsive gesture,

emphasizing her girlish nature, Bathsheba sends Boldwood a valentine. The puzzled neighbour soon discovers (from Gabriel) who sent this missive – and on becoming aware of her becomes attracted, spellbound and then entirely obsessed in rapid degrees.

At this point there enters on the scene the dashing scarlet-clad Sergeant Troy, a figure of compelling charm, energy and wit – epitomizing jaunty attractiveness and daring excitement. Having already captured the heart (and body) of Bathsheba's maidservant, the hapless Fanny Robin, Troy wins Bathsheba from both Boldwood and Oak.

But Troy's union with Bathsheba does not last. As the events unfold, each one told with a pressing inevitability laden with Hardian 'fatalism', Bathsheba is caught in the snare of her own misguided love, a trap made more

A patient shepherd
Gabriel has spent his whole life working towards his own sheep farm, when one night his over-enthusiastic dog chases his sheep off a cliff. He has to start again as Bathsheba's shepherd.

A girlish prank
On a dreary afternoon, on 13 February, Bathsheba and her servant Liddy send a valentine to Boldwood. The "off-hand" act has unforeseen consequences.

The farming life
(left) The events of the story are dominated by farm work. Bathsheba may be concerned about her effect on men, but her primary concern is always her farm.

Mistress and men
(below) At the annual "shearing-supper" Bathsheba sings her workers a ballad of as yet unrealized significance, about a soldier's love.

complex and difficult by the desperate unrequited passion of Boldwood and only relieved by the compassionate selflessness of Gabriel.

'A PASTORAL TALE'
Hardy called *Far From The Madding Crowd* 'a pastoral tale', and set the dramatic interplay of characters in an isolated rural community in the area he called, for the first time, Wessex. Although he draws on first-hand observations of his native Dorset, Hardy's poetic vision endows his landscape with a timelessness, a seasonal beauty and a poignant sense of tradition and rural continuity which seem to add a greater significance to the uneventful lives that are usually lived there – away from the "madding" (frenzied) crowd.

And it is these uneventful lives, inextricably tied to the never-ending cycle of the seasons, that inevitably remain after the transient sufferings and dramas in the story are over.

The characters of the local "workfolk" of Weatherbury form the Wessex equivalent of the Classical Greek 'Chorus' – re-emphasizing and ushering forward the action by their involvement in the scene and adding a comic relief which serves to make the dramas of the central characters more tragic and moving.

These rustic philosophers are at Warren's Malthouse, swigging cider around the fire when the news breaks that young Fanny Robin has gone missing. Their joint response is both comic in its expression and tragic in the awful accuracy of its prediction.
'O – 'tis burned – 'tis burned' came from Joseph Poorgrass's dry lips.
'No – 'tis drowned!' said Tall.
'Or 'tis her father's razor!' suggested Billy Smallbury with a vivid sense of detail.
After this, there is little doubt about the fate that awaits poor Fanny.

Apart from being a 'pastoral tale', *Far From The Madding Crowd* is at once a melodrama, a romance, a tragedy, and an explicit document of rural society. It was commissioned in 1873 as a monthly serial to appear in the popular and well-respected *Cornhill Magazine*. The magazine's editor, Leslie Stephen, asked for plenty of incidents 'to catch the attention of readers'. It is these powerful incidents, described with a poetic quality, that leave a lasting impression.

One of the most stunning episodes shows Troy dazzling Bathsheba with his virtuoso sword-play. The breath-taking pace, energy and hypnotic power of Troy's display are matched by Hardy's writing. The scene starts with the couple – he dressed in scarlet – in the golden evening light, facing each other on the "yielding" "carpet of moss", and Troy "producing the sword, which, as he raised it into the sunlight, gleamed a sort of greeting, like a living thing".

Troy then proceeds to 'cut and thrust' around Bathsheba, almost touching her with the sword's blade, but not quite, so that:

Beams of light caught from the low sun's rays, above, around, in front of her, well-nigh shut out earth and heaven – all emitted in the marvellous evolutions of Troy's reflecting blade, which seemed everywhere at once, and yet nowhere specially. These circling gleams were accompanied by a keen rush that was almost a whistling – also springing from all sides of her at once. In short, she was enclosed in a firmament of light, and of sharp hisses, resembling a sky-full of meteors close at hand . . . she could see the hue of Troy's sword arm, spread in a scarlet haze over the space covered by its motions . . . [until] his movements lapsed slower, and she could see them individually. The hissing of the sword ceased and he stopped entirely.

When Troy cuts a lock of her hair, and she realizes for the first time the deadly sharpness of the blade, "Bathsheba, overcome by a hundred tumultuous feelings resulting from

the scene, abstractedly sat down on a tuft of heather". And she is powerless to resist the "gentle dip of Troy's mouth downwards upon her own".

The sexual imagery of the scene is obvious and, as is apt for Sergeant Troy's relationship with Bathsheba, it is a thrilling, dangerous sort of sex. The love that Shepherd Gabriel bears Bathsheba is of a different kind entirely. His love shares the earthy sexuality to be found in Nature itself: "every pore was open, and every stalk was swollen with racing currents of juice". His farming skills extend such natural eroticism so that sheep-shearing and harvesting take on the significance of a shared intimacy with his 'mistress' Bathsheba.

Thus Hardy uses the countryside and rural pursuits not only as a realistic backdrop to the drama, but as a means of developing the emotional characters of the individuals.

His sensitive ears and eyes invest even simple rural scenes with a sacred quality where rustling leaves and freshening winds seem an animation of a mysterious and wonderful spirit. It is a spirit that is shared by the characters who people the landscape.

HARDY'S WEB

Hardy ties his events together in a way that gives the smallest accident of fortune, or inconsequential event, far greater significance. In *Far From The Madding Crowd* the plot is developed by almost incredible contrivances.

J. Ritchie: A Border Fair/Fine Art Photographic Library

L. Fildes: The Village Wedding. (Detail)/Christopher Wood Bridgeman Art Library

"*When the love-led man had ceased from his labours Bathsheba came and looked him in the face.*
'*Gabriel, will you stay on with me?' she said, smiling winningly, and not troubling to bring her lips quite together again at the end, because there was going to be another smile soon.*
'*I will,' said Gabriel.*"

A country wedding
(left) In the quietly joyful ending of the story, harmony is re-established: "Here's long life and happiness to neighbour Oak and his comely bride!"

Love in death
(right) Although Troy brutally rejects Fanny to marry Bathsheba, when he discovers his dead mistress and their dead child, he is devastated: "This woman is more to me, dead as she is than you were, or are, or can be."

Troy, for example, first meets Bathsheba in a 'Hardian accident' in which his spurs entangle in her dress in the dark of night when the couple pass each other; Gabriel comes to Upper Farm by chancing to see its hay ricks ablaze from a distance; on her intended wedding day, Fanny waits outside 'All Souls' church instead of 'All Saints' and so gives Troy an excuse to abandon her, and Boldwood's sexual obsession with Bathsheba is heralded by the spur-of-the-moment, thoughtless act of her sending him a valentine. By means of such incidents Hardy enmeshes all his characters in an intriguing web.

The plot itself is hinged around the most elemental and powerful of all human emotions – love. The destructive and creative power of this emotion unleashed in a tiny rural community creates the story itself. But a central theme, developed through Hardy's portrayal of love, is the need to confront reality and not escape into a romantic dream; a theme clearly and powerfully drawn in the character of Boldwood who loses all grip on reality as a result of his fatal obsession.

Bathsheba herself, a little older and a good deal wiser eventually comes down to earth, and on a damp Dorset morning marries the man whom she must inevitably marry. It is the rustic chorus, the age-old voice of common-sense that has the last word, and puts the drama in context:

'tis as 'tis, why, it might have been worse'.

At the sheep fair (above) Farmers and workfolk are entertained here by travelling players. One of them is Bathsheba's errant and long-lost husband Troy.

In the Background

'SCARLET FEVER'

Hardy was intrigued by a widespread phenomenon known in the 19th century as 'scarlet fever' – the passion evoked by soldiers among the women of England. In *Far From The Madding Crowd*, Sergeant Troy – dressed in scarlet uniform, and with a dashing, seductive manner – enters the little rural community, sweeps two women off their feet, then leaves "almost in a flash, like a brand swiftly waved".

Such stories – symbolizing the 'invasion' of the steady, rural scene by exciting foreign influences – were the basis of many popular ballads sung throughout agricultural communities. Bathsheba herself sings one of Hardy's favourites at the shearing-supper:

'For his bride a soldier sought her,
    And a winning tongue had he:
On the banks of Allan Water
    None was gay as she!'

Most of these ballads laid a moralizing emphasis, as Hardy's *Far From The Madding Crowd* does, on the sorrows that followed the brief pleasures to be enjoyed with the scarlet-clad gallants.

CHARACTERS IN FOCUS

In the small rural community depicted in *Far From The Madding Crowd,* the personal traits of the main characters – steadfastness, vanity, obsessiveness and charm – form the basis of the pastoral tragedy. The 'minor' characters – the workfolk of Weatherbury – all have their own idiosyncratic personalities, but Hardy presents them as part of the timeless, unchanging Wessex landscape and uses them to put the drama in context.

WHO'S WHO

Bathsheba Everdene A handsome young woman farmer. Though somewhat prone to vanity, she is never "deliberately a trifler for the affections of men".

Gabriel Oak A sheep farmer who suffers a tragedy and loses his farm, then goes to work for Bathsheba. He remains her faithful lover and supporter.

Sergeant Frank Troy A dashing young soldier, well-educated and dazzlingly expert at swordplay and womanizing. Essentially shallow, "He would speak of love and think of dinner".

Farmer William Boldwood Bathsheba's farmer neighbour whose apparent calmness turns to obsessive, destructive passion for her.

Fanny Robin Bathsheba's servant girl who is seduced and abandoned by Troy.

Pennyways A dishonest bailiff, dismissed by Bathsheba.

The Maltster Head of the Smallbury family and leader of the local drinking men. A man of indeterminate age, his own calculations make him 117.

Liddy Smallbury His great granddaughter, and Bathsheba's servant and confidante – a "light-hearted English country girl".

Jan Coggan A Weatherbury local, full of proverbial wisdom and cider.

Henerey Fray The grumpy would-be-bailiff who likes to look on the dark side of life.

Joseph Poorgrass A local farmhand, renowned for his shyness: "Twere, blush, blush, blush with me".

Laban Tall A man of such inconsequence that he is referred to as "Susan Tall's husband".

J.E. Millais: Effie Deans, Christies/Bridgeman Art Library

Little Fanny Robin, Bathsheba's "youngest servant" is seduced by Sergeant Troy and his promises of marriage, and runs away from the farm to follow him. A "slight and fragile creature", she inadvertently waits outside the wrong church on their intended wedding day, and so gives Troy the chance to abandon her and marry her rich mistress. Unknown to Troy, Fanny is pregnant and destitute. She and her baby die in the Casterbridge workhouse, and her body is brought home to Upper Farm for burial. It is only when she is dead that Troy faces up to the suffering he has caused her, and professes his love for her – declaring that "in the sight of Heaven, you are my very, very wife".

Dignified, middle-aged and reserved, (below) bachelor Farmer Boldwood does not notice Bathsheba until she sends him a valentine – an act that triggers a devastating, obsessive response. For despite his outward calm, Boldwood is "a hotbed of tropic intensity". "His equilibrium disturbed, he was in extremity at once. If an emotion possessed him at all, it ruled him . . . He was always hit mortally, or he was missed."

"Brilliant in brass and scarlet", Sergeant Troy (above) symbolizes the exciting outside forces which disrupt the steady flow of rural life: "His sudden appearance was to darkness what the sound of the trumpet is to silence". A charming talker, he captures hearts, but cannot face the responsibilities of love. " 'Treat them fairly, and you're a lost man,' he would say." He abandons both Fanny and Bathsheba – and his return to Weatherbury has fatal results.

Fine Art Photographics

The rustic philosophers (above) who meet at Warren's Malthouse to share cider, gossip and wise comments upon the goings-on in the village form a comic 'Chorus' to the main action.

Bathsheba Everdene's "bright face and dark hair", and her "bright air and manner" make a strong impression on the male farmers of Wessex, among whom she is "like a breeze among furnaces". The "keenly pointed corners of her red mouth" suggest potential for "alarming exploits of sex". Gabriel is devoted to her, Boldwood obsessed by her and Troy is enamoured by her beauty and money. But despite her impulsive nature, Bathsheba takes her farming seriously.

"An intensely humane man", Gabriel Oak (right) is also modest, honest and faithful as Bathsheba's shepherd and would-be husband: "I shall do one thing in this life – one thing certain – that is to love you, long for you and keep wanting you till I die", he tells her. Gabriel is uncommonly skilled as both shepherd and farmer – only he can save dying sheep and burning hayricks – and so deeply in touch with Nature that he tells the time by the stars, rather than by his eccentric clock.

DISTURBING TRUTHS

Hardy thought that novelists should deal honestly with what 'everybody is thinking but nobody is saying' – 'the relations of the sexes'. Some Victorian critics found such honesty little short of revolting.

Although he is renowned as one of the greatest of English novelists, Hardy wrote novels through necessity rather than choice. Poetry was his first love, and it was to poetry that he returned after 25 years. Writing novels, he realized at an early stage, was the only way to earn a living from literature.

His first attempt at fiction, *The Poor Man and the Lady* was rejected by the publisher Alexander Macmillan, 'the tendency of the writing being socialistic, not to say revolutionary'. Yet Macmillan recognized that this unknown writer had potentially great 'power and purpose', and recommended that Hardy should try the story with Chapman and Hall, Dickens' old publisher. There it was read by the novelist George Meredith who advised Hardy to abandon it, but encouraged him to write something with a 'purely artistic purpose, giving it a more complicated plot'.

M. Hobbema: The Avenue, Middelharnis, National Gallery, London

Harmony

(left) Like many of his contemporaries, Hardy had profound respect for the clear-sighted realism of the Dutch painters of the 17th century. This painting by Hobbema of the 'The Avenue, Middelharnis' was his favourite – in it Hardy saw the perfect blend of man and landscape that he emulated in his novels of 'character and environment'.

Fine Art Photographic Library

A Dorset study
From Max Gate (right), Hardy continued to draw on his native Dorset. As early as 1872, his work (below) was being shaped by rural life.

Sex was a word – let alone a subject – that no publisher of the time, if he wished to remain in business, dared mention. The silence over sex was helped by the publishing process itself. Weekly and monthly magazines dominated the market for fiction, and their editors and proprietors certainly wished to keep the lid on the nation's morals. *Harper's New Monthly Magazine* set the tone for many when it urged its contributors not to include anything 'which could not be read aloud in any family circle'.

Love and marriage, the two themes on which Hardy concentrated, were the two topics most likely to bring him into conflict with Victorian values. In his novels the havoc wreaked in human affairs by blind passion or an unwise marriage is explored in a way that was fresh and original and daring in its day. And as his relationship with his own wife became increasingly strained, Hardy even questioned marriage itself – the very cornerstone of Victorian society. In *Tess of the D'Urbervilles*, marriage is "an arbitary law of society which has no foundation in Nature", and in *Jude* it is seen as a "sordid contract based on material convenience".

Not surprisingly for an author with Hardy's preoccupations, he ran into difficulties. Leslie Stephen (Virginia Woolf's father), who was editor of the prestigious *Cornhill Magazine* which serialized *Far From The Madding Crowd*, was uneasy at Troy's seduction of Fanny Robin, and advised Hardy to treat the matter 'gingerly'. And when Fanny subsequently dies in childbirth in the workhouse,

This Hardy did, and in 1871, with the help of £75 out of his own pocket towards the cost of production, *Desperate Remedies* was published. Within a few weeks most of the 500 copies had been remaindered, and Hardy lost £15 in the venture.

Although the scenes of rural life were praised, as were Hardy's powers of natural description, most critics slated *Desperate Remedies'* sensational plot – murder, attempted rape, and violent sexual dreams – and they condemned certain scenes on the grounds of impropriety.

The ultra-sensitive Hardy took this response very much to heart. Such criticisms were to dog him for the rest of his career as a novelist, culminating in 1896 with the public burning of his latest novel, *Jude the Obscure* by a bishop of the Church of England.

THE STRONGEST PASSION

Hardy wrote 14 novels in all, and three volumes of short stories. They are all, in very different ways, love stories, and concern themselves with what Hardy calls in his Preface to *Jude*, 'the strongest passion known to humanity': sex.

Natural passion
(above) The staid morals of Victorian England were shaken by Hardy's explicit portrayals of sexuality – yet to Hardy, sexual passion was as natural as the rhythm of the seasons and the fecundity of Nature. Only when people lost touch with the land, he believed, was sex likely to lead to 'fret and fever, derision and disaster . . . in a deadly war between flesh and spirit'.

The new woman
(right) Hardy's novels are notable for their independent, spirited women, who never lose their desire to "be loved to madness".

F. Morgan: The Rivals (Detail)/Bridgeman Art Library

The outsiders

(left) In Hardy's tales, outsiders often intrude upon the closed rural community to disrupt the timeless nature of country customs. Passing soldiers shatter the calm to dally with the village girls and upset the tranquil pattern of relationships. Hardy witnessed these, and other intrusions slowly eroding traditional rural life – the conflicts form recurrent themes in his novels.

of the things that convinced him of this was the suicide of his brilliant friend and mentor Horace Moule, which happened when Hardy was a third of the way through *Far From The Madding Crowd*. He was devastated. The tragic figure of Boldwood was his immediate response to Moule's death, and afterwards all his heroes and heroines are doomed to failure and despair.

A GROWING PESSIMISM

Over the 21 years that separates *Far From The Madding Crowd* from Hardy's last novel *Jude the Obscure*, he shows a growing pessimism. *Far From The Madding Crowd* ends in marriage, happiness and harmony. The ending of *Jude* could not be more grim. After Jude's son 'Little Father Time' has killed his half-brothers and then himself, Jude reflects upon "the coming universal wish, unknown to the last generation, not to live".

Hardy's later heroines and heroes such as Tess and Jude are conspicuously alone. They are individuals isolated from the rest of society because they reject conventional patterns of behaviour and belief. Tess has borne an illegitimate baby; Jude lives in unmarried union with his cousin Sue. All three are doomed to suffer because they dare to challenge accepted conventions.

But the tragedy of Jude (and Tess) is not just a result of their breaking of society's rules; they have both broken away from their roots, left the rural communities of their birth, and so lost touch with Nature. And for Hardy, once humans break their sustaining links with the natural world, they are doomed. For the beautiful Wessex countryside that pervades his novels is not simply a picturesque backdrop for his stories, it is part of the mysterious energy of Nature, whose rhythm is the rhythm of life itself.

he wrote asking Hardy whether it might not be better 'to omit the baby' altogether. But Stephen conceded that his demand for changes was the result of 'an excessive prudery of which I am ashamed'.

Other editors were less understanding. When Hardy presented Edward Arnold, editor of *Murray's Magazine* with the manuscript of *Tess of the D'Urbervilles* in 1889, he could barely conceal his feeling of outrage. Returning the story he said, 'I know well enough that these tragedies are being played out every day in our midst, but I believe the less publicity they have the better'.

CENSORING THE TEXT

Hardy became adept at preparing his original text for publication in 'censored' form for weekly or monthly magazines. When *Tess* appeared in *The Graphic* in July 1891, it had been much 'mutilated', he said, as a concession to conventionality – a piece of work that he had carried out with a certain 'cynical amusement'.

Sometimes the changes Hardy was asked to make where minimal. In *The Trumpet Major*, for example, he was advised to move a lover's meeting from a Sunday to a Saturday. Other changes were far-reaching and ridiculous. When *Jude the Obscure* first appeared in a bowdlerized version in *Harper's* under the title *Hearts Insurgent*, the word 'couch' was substituted for 'bed', 'sex' was changed to 'affection', and even 'kissing' was replaced by 'shaking hands'.

Hardy wrote 12 novels for serialization, and the demand of editors for a strong plot with plenty of incident certainly led him to introduce characters and events somewhat gratuitously at times. Some of the coinci-

dences upon which his plots depend are partly the result of the over-extended narrative demanded by the method of publication. But they also reflect Hardy's strong belief in Fate.

In his later novels – after *Far From The Madding Crowd* – Hardy never seems to tire of inventing awful twists of Fate that lead his heroes and heroines inexorably towards despair and doom. And even in that novel, the outwardly calm Boldwood – for whom the slightest careless act (Bathsheba's valentine) could tip the balance into chaos – prefigures the tragic characters of his later works.

Sometimes Hardy's fateful coincidences are so devastating that it seems as if the author is loading the dice against his heroes to an incredible extent. But Hardy was convinced that such things (or worse) did happen. One

Living landscape

(right) The stirring Wessex countryside is much more than an idealized setting for the display of its rustic characters – it is a living landscape to which humans must be bound if they are to prosper. Those who lack sympathy and awe for Nature are cut off from the rhythm of life, and are doomed to failure and despair – a despair Hardy believed must become ever more common as people move away from the land.

WORKS·IN OUTLINE

Author of 14 novels and many short stories, Thomas Hardy was both the greatest chronicler and dramatist of English country life. But his career as a novelist ended abruptly in 1896, when the public burning of his last and darkest novel persuaded him to give up fiction altogether.

Hardy divided his work into three categories: Novels of Character and Environment; Romances and Fantasies; and Novels of Ingenuity. All his greatest books are Novels of Character and Environment, which explore the close bond between people and landscape in his beautiful 'Wessex' countryside.

Hardy achieved his first success with the charming rustic idyll *Under the Greenwood Tree* (1872). *The Trumpet Major* (1880), a novel of Romance and Fantasy, was in a more light-hearted vein than the sombre Wessex tales – *The Return of the Native* (1878), *The Mayor of Casterbridge* (1886) and *The Woodlanders* 1887). These novels enhanced his reputation, but the outraged response to *Jude the Obscure* (1896) brought him notoriety to match his fame.

G.B. O'Neil: A Statute Fair/Fine Art Photographic Library

BBC Hulton Picture Library

THE MAYOR OF CASTERBRIDGE
◆ 1886 ◆

Michael Henchard, a hay-trusser, gets drunk at Weyhill Fair and offers his wife and child for sale along the road – until a passing sailor, Newson, buys them for five guineas. Appalled by what he·has done, Henchard pledges not to drink for 20 years. Thus begins the tragic tale of the hay-trusser who becomes Mayor of Casterbridge – one of Hardy's most powerful stories.

At first, all goes well for Henchard. He becomes a prosperous hay-merchant, and Mayor of Casterbridge. Then, after 18 years, his wife returns, bringing a child, Elizabeth-Jane. But Fate, and his own granite nature, conspire against him, and from the moment he quarrels with his capable assistant Donald Farfrae, he is doomed, losing everything to Farfrae. When his selling of his wife becomes common knowledge, proud Henchard's ruin is complete. He takes to drinking again, comforted by Elizabeth-Jane, now revealed to be Newson's daughter. When Newson returns to reclaim his daughter, Henchard dies in despair.

The doomed figure of Henchard bestrides the novel like a colossus, and he is perhaps Hardy's finest creation – a great, blind bull of a man, as rigid and strong as an Old Testament prophet – and the story of his downfall has few parallels in English literature after Shakespeare's Macbeth.

T. Webster: Practising for a Village Concert/Christie's/Bridgeman Art Library

UNDER THE GREENWOOD TREE

✦ 1872 ✦

Dick Dewy and Fancy Day (right) are the lovers at the heart of Hardy's idyllic rural tale. *Under the Greenwood Tree* was Hardy's second novel, and the book that established him as an outstanding author. It is the most rustic of all his stories, drawing heavily on his intimate knowledge of Dorset country life. Dick is the son of the local 'tranter' or carrier, while Fancy is the pretty young village schoolmistress, and their romance is played out against an endearing portrait of village folk in 'Mellstock'. The book is full of rustic characters – most memorably and humorously the Mellstock 'quire' or choir, whose exploits to prevent a new-fangled organ replacing them in the local church no doubt recall Hardy's days playing the fiddle with his father in church and at agricultural functions.

M. Stone: Courtship (Detail) Fine Art Photographic

THE RETURN OF THE NATIVE

✦ 1878 ✦

The Wilderness of Egdon Heath (right) lying between Poole and Wareham in Dorset, provides a sombre, brooding backdrop for the passionate love stories played out in this gripping tale. This landscape, peopled with rustics living as they have for centuries, and the slow, deliberate pace of the novel conveys a sense of timelessness and inevitability. There are undertones of Greek tragedy, the story originally being planned as five sections, each corresponding to a scene in a play and the action taking place over a year and a day. Hardy explores the theme of the return of the native (Clym Yeobright) with new ideas – his idealistic aims having little bearing on the daily existence of the locals. The emotional and rebellious Eustacia Vye is one of Hardy's most exotic and memorable characters. Her desire for Clym is fuelled mainly by a desire to escape from the Heath, which to her is oppressive and confining, to a larger, more glamorous world – a world of "music, poetry, passion and war". Her disillusionment when she finds Clym content to remain a humble peasant, and the effect of this on the lives and passions interwoven with theirs, ultimately lead to tragedy, showing the impossibility of change or escape.

THE TRUMPET MAJOR

✦ 1880 ✦

The Trumpet Major is classed as one of Hardy's romances and fantasies, and arose from research Hardy had done for his ambitious verse-drama, *The Dynasts* on the theme of the Napoleonic wars. The novel opens and closes with a celebratory supper at Overcombe Mill, and in between there is a triangular love courtship in an idyllic setting against a background of a threatened Napoleonic invasion. Anne Garland, a lovely local girl, is pursued by three suitors, the two miller's sons – John and Bob Loveday – and Festus Derriman, the coarse yeoman, whose limited appeal arises mainly from his social standing. John Loveday is the Trumpet Major of the title; a principled and reflective soul, his love for Anne fails to arouse a like response in her. Although in time, with greater self-knowledge gained through misfortune, she comes to appreciate his virtues, her passions are aroused by his brother, Bob – a generous, light-hearted but feckless sailor. The novel is resolved when John, seeing Anne's true feelings, gives up all claim to her and, as described by Hardy in a moving passage, leaves into the darkness "to blow his trumpet till silenced for ever upon one of the bloody battle-fields of Spain."

E. Landseer: Landscape, Roy Miles Fine Painting/Bridgeman Art Library

THE WOODLANDERS
◆ 1887 ◆

Wooded country at the edge of Blackmoore Vale (right) provides the setting for this atmospheric country tale, which is also a bitter attack on a society hemmed in by petty morality and dogged by status-seeking. Similar in many ways to *Far From The Madding Crowd*, it tells of the doomed love of honest forester Giles Winterbourne for Grace Melbury who, once educated, marries doctor Edred Fitzpiers instead. Giles is comforted by the devotion of simple village girl Marty South, but still pines for Grace. When Fitzpiers proves unfaithful and Grace flees to Gile's woodland cottage, he readily takes her in, moving out respectfully to a primitive shelter, where he dies of exposure. Grace returns to Fitzpiers and Marty is left to mourn alone. Hardy wrote of *The Woodlanders*, 'I think I like it, *as a story*, best of all.'

Fine Art Photographic Library

JUDE THE OBSCURE
◆ 1896 ◆

Jude Fawley (below) is the stonemason at the centre of Hardy's final novel, whose intellectual and spiritual aspirations bring him ultimately to despair and death. Unlike the other novels, *Jude* has a contemporary setting and Hardy abandons his usual rustic backcloth to create his own bleak vision of a modern man and, in Sue Bridehead, a modern woman – 'an intellectualized, emancipated bundle of nerves'. Dubbed 'Jude the Obscene' by those outraged by its sexual content and its criticisms of marriage, *Jude* was Hardy's most controversial work. Some believe it to be his most powerful and impressive.

Mary Evans Picture Library

Hardy's Wessex

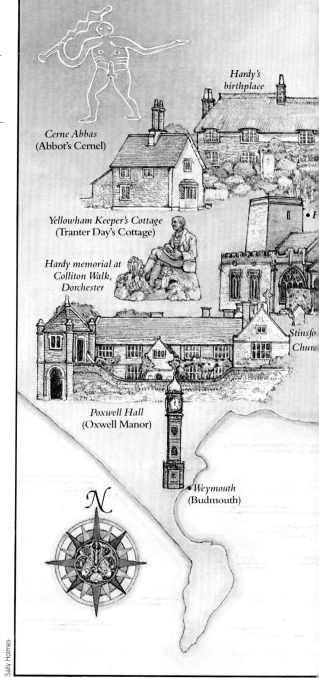

Cerne Abbas
(Abbot's Cernel)

Hardy's
birthplace

Yellowham Keeper's Cottage
(Tranter Day's Cottage)

Hardy memorial at
Colliton Walk,
Dorchester

Stinsfo
Chure

Poxwell Hall
(Oxwell Manor)

Weymouth
(Budmouth)

N

Sally Holmes

An amalgam of an ancient West Saxon kingdom and his own native Dorset cast the mould for Hardy's 'Wessex'. It both harnessed and released his imagination.

Higher Bockhampton lies three miles east of Dorchester, the county town of Dorset. At the end of a narrow lane, known as Cherry Alley, stands a "long low cottage" with a "hipped roof of thatch", tucked between "a heath and a wood". Built in 1800 by the novelist's great-grandfather, it is known simply as 'Hardy's Cottage'. In the autumn of 1873, Thomas Hardy III, was living here with his parents, helping with the cider-making and immersed in writing *Far From The Madding Crowd*. In the novel, cottages such as this punctuate the 'Weatherbury' landscape like beacons.

Inspired by scenes familiar to him from childhood, Hardy continually drew on the Dorset countryside, his family and neighbours in writing the book. Almost every scene or setting was based on personal experience – incidents of local life recollected and recounted to him by his mother, or on his own close observation of nature and people during this period. His diary entry on 4th November records a thunder-storm at Bockhampton. 'The light is greenish and unnatural . . . A silver fringe hangs from the eaves of the house to the ground.' In Chapter 37 of *Far From The Madding Crowd*, "The Storm – The Two Together", in which Gabriel Oak and Bathsheba Everdene protect the ricks from the storm, the lightning is "emerald" and the rain comes "in liquid spines, unbroken in continuity".

As he matured as a novelist, Hardy came to realize that Dorset was almost his sole source of inspiration. He needed 'to be actually among the people described at the time of describing them'. Away from his roots he felt isolated and ill at ease and his novel-writing became stilted, stale and conventional.

PART REAL, PART DREAM

The first time Hardy uses the term 'Wessex' to describe the area in which his forebears had lived for centuries is in the opening sentence of Chapter 50 in *Far From The Madding Crowd*. In 1895 he described his reasons for adopting the term; 'The series of novels I projected', he wrote, 'being mainly of the kind called local . . . seemed to require a territorial definition of some sort to lend unity to their scene. Finding that the area of a single county did not afford a canvas large enough for this purpose, and that there were objections to an invented name, I disinterred the old one [the ancient kingdom of the West Saxons]. The region designated was known but vaguely'. It is hardly surprising, then, that ancient monuments loom large in his novels or that a strong sense of history pervades every village and landscape.

A familiar landscape
(right) Hardy created a semi-fictional world, with a consistent system of place names, and applying it to a real geographical area — his native Dorset. A tourist attraction in his own lifetime, Dorchester ('Casterbridge') was the heart of 'Wessex', but his characters roam over a wider realm of six 'counties' (inset).

'things were like that'
(below) The novelist drew on scenes familiar to him since childhood and took great pains to ensure authenticity. Intimate observation of agricultural activities and customs gave his descriptions a pungent realism. But the inhabitants 'engaged in certain occupations . . . just as they are shown doing . . .'

THOMAS HARDY

The Turberville Window
• *Bere Regis*
(Kingsbere)

khampton
llstock)

Egdon Heath

Lulworth Cove
(Lulwind/Lulstead)

Durdle Dor

Oxford •

• *Stonehenge*

Shaftesbury •

• *Dorchester*

• *Corfe Castle*

An ancient kingdom
(left) In Hardy's time,
Dorset was 'known but
vaguely' to the outside
world, yet the landscape bore
all the signs of a history
stretching back to pagan
times. Stonehenge remains
as a monument to it,
and appears as a potent
symbol in Tess of the
D'Urbervilles.

This 'partly real, partly dream-country' covered an area larger than that of the county of Dorset and, as Hardy suggests, was closer to ancient Wessex in consisting of six counties: Berkshire ("North Wessex"); Hampshire ("Upper Wessex"); Wiltshire ("Mid-Wessex"); Dorset ("South Wessex"); Somerset ("Outer Wessex"); and Devon ("Lower Wessex"). Cornwall is adjacent and is referred to as "Off Wessex".

Though Hardy draws on this large and, in his day, remote area, all his major novels, with the exception of *Jude the Obscure*, are set in the county of Dorset. And most of these concentrate on the even smaller area immediately surrounding Dorchester.

SEEKING AN IDENTITY

Thomas Hardy applied his own system of place names to a fictional area based on fact. He did so comprehensively and, in most cases, consistently.

To help his readers identify the real place names he had disguised, Hardy produced a map of Wessex complete with 'county' boundaries, natural features, coastal resorts, towns, villages and hamlets. This attempt at lending reality to a fictional world was taken to extreme lengths and became a source of amusement to him.

In a Preface to *The Woodlanders* of April 1912, he says that though honoured by the many inquiries 'for the true name and exact location of the hamlet 'Little Hintock', in which the greater part of the action of this story goes on', he has to confess he does not know himself exactly where it is. However, 'to oblige readers', he once spent 'several hours on a bicycle with a friend in a serious attempt to discover the real spot'; but the search ended in failure, though tourists assured him 'that they have found it without trouble, and that it answers in every particular to the description given'.

EXTENDING THE BOUNDARIES

Despite the amusement he derived from his creation, it is evident that 'Wessex' took on a shape and form that extended the boundaries of his real world.

Once created, the fictional name for a real place in one book was usually carried over to another. The 'Weatherbury' in *Far From The Madding Crowd* appears throughout the Wessex novels as the name of Puddletown, or Piddletown as it was called before the reign of Queen Victoria.

If it all started in a casual way, Hardy soon became identified with his own creation. 'Hardy's Wessex' became popular and the press was quick to cash in on the phrase. By 1895, as Hardy himself says, the public was happy to accept 'the anachronism of a Wessex

Timeless characters
(above) Many inhabitants of
Hardy's Dorset relied upon
an orally transmitted
knowledge and wisdom, and
were resistant to change
imposed from the outside
world. Time itself takes on
a different quality in Hardy's
dramas of country life; "Ten
generations failed to alter the
turn of a single phrase".

Corfe Castle
(left) Though picturesque,
Hardy's settings were not
sentimentalized – real
hardship and abject poverty
were too evident during the
agricultural depression. At
Corfe Castle in 1868, for
example, a family of eight
lived in an outhouse built for
a calf. Hardy called the castle
ruins 'Corvsgate'.

Ed Buziak

Stevens-Cox, Toucan Press, Guernsey

Ed Buziak

population living under Queen Victoria; – a modern Wessex of railways, the penny post, mowing and reaping machines, union workhouses, lucifer matches, labourers who could read and write, and National school children'.

'Wessex' both released and harnessed his imagination. Using imagined names gave Hardy greater freedom and saved causing offence to the inhabitants of real-life places. For despite being an imagined world, the Wessex novels contain descriptions of life in the region which are completely authentic. Indeed, Hardy was at pains to impress on his readers the accuracy of his portrait. 'At the date represented in the various narratives things were like that in Wessex', he wrote in his 'General Preface to the Novels and Poems'.

The Wessex depicted in Hardy's novels spans almost the whole of the 19th century – from the Napoleonic Wars at the beginning of the century (the setting of

The Trumpet Major) to the 1890s of *Jude The Obscure*. Throughout this period the south-west of England, and Dorset in particular, remained relatively remote and, to the visitor from London, old-fashioned. Indeed, there were few visitors to the region from other parts of the country until the last decade of the century. The railway only reached Dorchester in 1847, when Hardy was seven. Hardy's earliest memories were of 'men in the stocks, corn-law agitations, mail-coaches, road-waggons, tinder-boxes and candle-snuffing'.

During Hardy's lifetime the character of the county changed profoundly. The coming of the railways killed off, according to him, 'the orally transmitted ditties of centuries, being slain at a stroke by the London comic songs that were introduced'. But more was to change than the folk songs he so loved.

GRIM REALITY

Condemned, for the most part, to a life of poverty and squalor, the farm labourers of Dorset – among whom Hardy could count close cousins and uncles – were the worst paid and worst housed in the country. In the 1840s the average wage of the Dorset labourer was a pitiful 7s 6d a week – lower than in any other county in England. Hardy grew up acutely aware of

A rural community
(above) The farming seasons bound rural communities together in shared labour – and in the traditional festivities and observances.

Old Harry Rocks
(top) Dorset's scenic coastline features in many Hardy novels. His fictional place names echo now-forgotten folklore elements.

the poverty and pain experienced by so many – and witnessed events he was never to forget. 'As a child I knew by sight a sheep-keeping boy who, to my horror, shortly afterwards died of want, the contents of his stomach at the autopsy being raw turnip only.'

While life for those in work was hard – Alexander Somerville in his *The Whistler at the Plough* (1852) recalls 'rising at four in the morning and coming home and supper at seven in the evening' – for those without work, life was a desperate struggle for survival. The workhouse was often the final degrading step.

Finding work was itself a precarious business and depended in many parts of Dorset on the hiring fairs held each year on 14 February. Here the young Hardy saw men standing around dressed in "smock-frocks and gaiters, the shepherds with their crooks, the carters with a zone of whipcord round their hats, thatchers with a straw tucked into the brim . . . in search for a new master". The ruined farmer in *Far From The Madding Crowd*, Gabriel Oak, is forced to seek a master in just such a setting.

HARSH LABOUR

To maintain a reasonable family income, the women and children also sought work on the land. A *Royal Commission on the Employment of Children, Young Persons and Women in Agriculture* of 1868, reported that as late as 1867 children under the age of six were working in the fields of Dorset. Sometimes whole families could be found engaged in farm labour. According to the *Victoria County History of Dorset*, 'not only was the labourer expected to work, but his wife, or at least his daughter, were dragged off into full work, and the boys were taken away too early from school'.

The Royal Commission also commented on 'the bad moral effects' on young girls of 'employment in field labour' – an effect Hardy chronicled in the plight of Tess Durbeyfield, "a fieldwoman pure and simple". Her fellow workers are the "dark virago, Car Darch, dubbed Queen of Spades", and "Nancy her sister, nicknamed the Queen of Diamonds". For the innocent Tess they are "a whorage". In real life, coarsened by "starvation, disease, degradation, death", release came in weekly bouts of drunkenness. Illegitimacy was a common result and marriage was too often a contract between unwilling partners hastily arranged before the birth of a child.

To the Victorian moral conscience the life of the rural poor was shocking. At village social gatherings, such as that reported in *The Times* of 3 August 1846, 'scenes (were) enacted which can at least rival, if not exceed, the disgusting orgies of antiquity'.

CHALLENGING THE IDYLL

Few writers honestly portrayed the countryside and the lives of those who worked on the land. Nostalgia for a idyllic past was the typical attitude of many 19th-century 'country' writers. Alone among the major novelists of his time, Hardy was an unsentimental countryman, who knew from first-hand observation the realities of rural life. He knew the countryside too well to share the picture of 'Merry England' conjured up in London publishing houses and endorsed by people whom he felt should have known better.

Though he lamented the passing of many aspects of traditional rural life, especially the crafts and the folk-tales passed down from generation to generation by word of mouth, he welcomed the improvements in the standard of living of the farm worker achieved in his lifetime. But, though these were 'changes at which we must rejoice', he saw that they also 'brought other changes which [were] not so attractive'. Thus the modern labourer had 'a less intimate and kindly relationship with the land' than that of Gabriel Oak. With the material progress that came later in the century came the values of the town, which for Hardy were in conflict with those of the countryside. Invariably in his novels from *Far From The Madding Crowd* on, it is the arrival of a town-based, or city-educated individual who disrupts and brings misery to the lives of the villagers.

With state education available to all after 1870, the local dialect declined and died. Tess is typical of her generation in speaking "two languages, the dialect at home, more or less; ordinary English abroad and to persons of quality". In its traditional form, local Dorset dialect as spoken by Grammer Oliver in *The Woodlanders* was close to German with expressions such as "ch woll", or "Ich woll", for "I will".

Real rusticity
(right) During Hardy's lifetime, the Dorset countryside was dotted with colourful tradesmen, such as this spar maker of Tolpuddle in the 1880s. Marty South in The Woodlanders *plies a similar trade. Other trades that appear in Hardy's work include 'reddlemen', furze cutters, pole-, peg- and hurdle-makers, heathcroppers, pig killers and a host of casual farm labourers who were able, like ex-farmer Gabriel Oak in* Far From The Madding Crowd, *to turn their hands to most tasks.*

Undisturbed calm
(above) Tranquil scenes such as this capture the atmosphere of the Wessex landscape as dusk approached. But the more distant future cast shadows of a more threatening kind – the traditional way of life was gradually eroded as the outside world encroached on 'anachronistic' Dorset.

Farm buildings
(left) In his novels, Hardy's buildings literally crumble with antiquity. Few, like this tithe barn at Abbotsbury, survive.

By the end of his life Hardy's Wessex had become a tourist attraction, aided by the publication of numerous books of topography of which the most thorough was *Hardy's Wessex* – a work in which Hardy himself had a hand – by his friend Hermann Lea. It was a painstaking reconstruction of every place mentioned in the 'Wessex novels' and contained a large collection of locations and buildings – some of which can still be seen, but many of which no longer stand – that Hardy describes in his text.

But 'Wessex', that region 'bounded on the north side by the Thames, on the south side by the English Channel, on the east by a line running from Hayling Island to Windsor Forest, and on the west by the Cornish coast', as he described it in 1912, was more than a geographical location. It was also 'any and every place' where 'these imperfect little dramas of country life and passions', as he modestly called his novels, were enacted.

TESS OF THE D'URBERVILLES

A powerfully moral book, *Tess* shocked Victorian readers because it criticized male crimes of seduction and hypocrisy and asserted a 'fallen' woman's purity.

In *Tess of the d'Urbervilles*, Hardy creates a timeless heroine on a scale as huge as the West Country landscape in which she moves. Tess's decline and fall is described with a passionate intensity of detail unequalled in any of Hardy's other novels.

The character of Tess is invested with all the qualities which Hardy felt to be most perfect, admirable and ultimately tragic in womankind. She is the most memorable of all his characters; we can hear her breathe and talk, we can see her walk down the maze of country lanes that form her destiny. In the Preface to *Tess*, Hardy wrote 'a novel is an impression, not an argument'. That may have been his intention, but through his portrayal of Tess we are also presented with a plea for compassion which is too powerful to refuse.

GUIDE TO THE PLOT

Tess of the d'Urbervilles is a story of a 'fine and picturesque country girl' who is forced to support her unfortunate and foolish parents. Her family is so poor that when her father, John Durbeyfield, learns about his noble ancestry it seems like a gift from heaven. Encouraged by his wife, he packs Tess off to lay kinship claims on the wealthy Stoke d'Urbervilles. Reluctantly, Tess agrees, but it proves to be her downfall. With her innocence and simple rural ways she is ill-equipped to deal with the worldly attentions of Alec d'Urberville. Struck by her beauty, Alec is only too pleased to call Tess 'cousin' in order to keep her near him. The Stoke d'Urbervilles actually bear no relation to the ancient d'Urberville family, but Alec deliberately misleads Tess in order to have his way with her. He takes advantage of her innocence and financial dependence and robs her of her maidenhood.

Within a short time of leaving home, Tess is back in her village, dishonoured and despairing. "O mother, my mother!" she cries, "How could I be expected to know? I was a child when I left the house four months ago. Why didn't you tell me there was danger in men-folk?" A baby girl is born whom she names 'Sorrow', but Sorrow dies after some months and Tess is plunged even further into despair. She struggles on, continuing to work as a field hand before taking a job as a milkmaid at the far-off Talbothays dairy.

Her summer at the dairy proves to be her happiest. There she meets Angel Clare, a

F. Walker: Autumn. Victoria & Albert Museum/Bridgeman Art Library

William Mulready: Off to Market. Christie's, London/Bridgeman Art Library

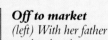

Off to market
(left) With her father too drunk to be roused, Tess agrees to go to market for him, with her younger brother. But the journey is ill-fated since their precious horse, Prince, is killed en route.

D'Urberville farm
(right) On arriving at the border of the estate, "the crimson brick lodge came first in sight, up to its eaves in dense evergreens," and "simple Tess Durbeyfield stood at a gaze, in a half-alarmed attitude, on the edge of the gravel sweep."

E.W. Waite: The Hatch Farm/Bridgeman Art Library

Youthful dreams
Before her fateful encounter with Alec d'Urberville, Tess (left) was "a fine and picturesque country girl, and no more." "Phases of her childhood lurked in her aspect still . . . For all her bouncing handsome womanliness, you could sometimes see her twelfth year in her cheeks, or her ninth sparkling from her eyes; and even her fifth would flit over the curves of her mouth now and then." But the innocence was all too soon to be lost, and it would be some time before a look of happiness would return to her face.

clergyman's son, who has decided to become a farmer and needs the experience of learning a dairyman's skills. Angel, the soft-spoken gentleman in the midst of simple country-folk, becomes fascinated by Tess and recognizes in her qualities which set her apart from the others. He sees in her the essence of pure, innocent womanhood and grows convinced, moreover, that she would also make a perfect farmer's wife.

For Tess, Angel is the love of her life. Her strength of feeling for him causes her an agony of conflict – is she worthy of being such a fine man's wife? She tries to refuse him but he will not hear of it. Then she tries to tell him about her seduction and she fails. Eventually, believing Angel Clare's love for her to be stronger than conventional morality, she marries him, and on their wedding night tells him about Alec and the baby. Angel is thunderstruck – "the woman I have been loving is not you" – and cannot forgive her. He leaves Tess, to try his fortune at farming in Brazil.

Tess is utterly crushed. She gives his small allowance of money to her family, who are poorer than ever, and is forced to search for work far afield to survive the winter. As things go from bad to worse for Tess, both the men in her life return, and the sense of impending doom builds up gradually but relentlessly to reach its inevitable conclusion.

A TRAGEDY

Tess is one of the great tragic heroines of 19th-century literature. From the opening chapters of the novel she is an innocent suffering at the indifferent hands of Fate. There are points in the story when it is clear that a different action on her part would almost certainly improve

"Thus the thing began. Had she perceived this meeting's import she might have asked why she was doomed to be seen and coveted that day by the wrong man, and not by some other man, the right and desired one . . ."

BBC Hutton Picture Library

Unwanted advances
(above right) Rescued by Alec from a rowdy late night dance, Tess finds herself alone with her 'protector'. "What am I, to be repulsed so by a mere chit like you?" he asks. And though she rejects his advances, he ignores all but his own desires.

The aftermath
(right) Left with a baby to tend, Tess tries to put the past behind her and, after a period of venturing out only at night, takes her place alongside other young girls in the corn fields.

Alexander Mann: The Gleaners (detail). Fine Art Society, London/Bridgeman

J.L. Van Kuyck: The Cow Shed, Josef Mensing Gallery/Bridgeman

her circumstances, but for Tess to be opportunist would be out of character. She is described throughout the novel as a creature of flight, always on the move, forced to seek rest in ever decreasing circles. At times she resembles a defenceless bird *"with the hopeless defiance of the sparrow's gaze . . ."* until at the end *"her breathing now was quick and small, like that of a lesser creature than a woman."*

It is as if there is something fundamentally wrong in the scheme of things which makes it impossible for Tess to live happily in the world. Although her poverty puts her at a disadvantage from the start, it is the cruel twists of Fate which repeatedly deny her any chance of happiness. She accepts favours from Alec d'Urberville only when to refuse would mean her family would starve. But Hardy's main concern in telling the story of *Tess* was not to make a statement about the economic hardship of rural life; what he was interested in was the clash between positive and negative life forces. He felt strongly that farm labourers were by definition closest to the life-affirming elements he worshipped. It is a lesson which Angel Clare, the gentleman playing at farmer, learns at Talbothays dairy:

"He grew away from old associations, and saw something new in life and humanity. Secondarily, he made close acquaintance with phenomena which he had before known but darkly – the seasons in their moods, morning and evening, night and noon, winds in their different tempers, trees, waters and mists, shades and silences, and the voices of inanimate things."

Tess already knows all this, at least on a subconscious level, which to Hardy's mind

Talbothays dairy
(above) "Tess had never in her recent life been so happy as she was now, possibly never would be so happy again. She was . . . physically and mentally suited among these new surroundings."

Emminster vicarage
(left) With no word from her husband Angel for months, Tess sets out to find Angel's father. But, having made the arduous 15-mile journey on foot, Tess loses her nerve when she overhears his brothers, fresh from morning worship, talking about his "ill-considered marriage".

Hard labour
Abandoned by Angel, Tess meets up with her old friend Marian and secures a place at Flintcomb-Ash farm (right). But it is a gruelling existence, "they worked on hour after hour . . . not thinking of the . . . injustice of their lot."

John White: A Village Wedding, Royal Albert Memorial Museum, Exeter/Bridgeman

W.P.A. Wells: Potato Pickers/Fine Art Photographic Library

> *"I am the same woman, Angel, as you fell in love with; yes, the very same! – not the one you disliked but never saw. What was the past to me as soon as I met you? It was a dead thing altogether."*

was far more valuable. Angel is deeply attracted to this quality in her but makes the mistake of idealizing her into *"a visionary essence of woman"*, not seeing the real Tess at all. At the crucial point where she tells him about Alec, he feels his dream has been destroyed and with it his love. Tess cries out: *"I thought, Angel, that you loved me – me, my very self! If it is I you do love, O how can it be that you look and speak so? It frightens me! Having begun to love you, I love you for ever – in all changes, in all disgraces, because you are yourself. I ask no more. Then how can you, O my husband, stop loving me?"*

This is Tess's tragedy; she moves in a world where insensitivity, coarseness and greed make it impossible for her to live as she should. Alec's baseness is easy to understand. Angel's rejection of her is much harder to forgive, and yet she forgives him and continues to love him through all her trials. It is Tess who possesses true compassion and generosity of spirit, unlike the 'gentlefolk' whose paths she crosses, and it is this which ennobles her suffering to make her story into an epic tragedy.

'A PURE WOMAN'

Hardy added the subtitle 'A Pure Woman', 'at the last moment, after reading the final proofs, as being the estimate left in a candid mind of the heroine's character – an estimate that nobody would be likely to dispute.' He could not have been more wrong: it was the addition of this subtitle that helped stir the controversy surrounding the book when it was first published in 1891. The many references to sex and physical passion were bound to offend Victorian morality, but then to insist that Tess who, having borne an illegitimate child, should still remain 'pure' was more than many critics could stand.

On this point however, Hardy is firm. Throughout the novel he emphasizes Tess's essential purity, asking that she should not be judged by her label of 'fallen woman', but instead be seen in her entirety against the landscape and circumstances of her birth. Hardy has created a wholly consistent character in Tess, where all her behaviour and responses to situations are in keeping with her nature. When she leaves Alec d'Urberville to return to her family, knowing the disgrace that faces her, she still refuses to accept his material support:

"I have said I will not take anything more from you, and I will not – I cannot! I should be your creature to go on doing that, and I won't!"

Tess is undeniably *good* where others are *bad* or sinful or weak. She is not without pride or vanity or passion, but her closeness to Nature, and her innocence, integrity and honesty, make her, in Hardy's opinion, blameless – while others are at fault.

The novel can be seen in a number of lights – as an attack on corruption, as a eulogy for the natural world, and a plea for a fairer treatment of women. Contemporary readers took up what they saw as Hardy's challenge to conventional views on sexual relations, discussing Tess's character across the dinner table. Hardy was more concerned to show Tess as a perfect image of woman's love:

"Clare did not know at that time the full depth of her devotion, its singlemindedness, its meekness; what endurance, what good faith."

Angel Clare learns too late what he once refused to see in her. As he and Tess journey towards an untimely end, Tess can think of little except her immediate happiness at being with him again:

"To her he was, as of old, all that was perfection, personally and mentally . . . his sickly face was beautiful as the morning to her affectionate regard on this day no less than when she first beheld him; for was it not the face of the one man on earth who had loved her purely, and who had believed in her as pure."

It is this quality, her unsullied devotion and love, that Hardy invites us to admire in Tess, and in so doing, forgive what the Victorians would have viewed as her 'sins'.

In the Background

MARKET FAIRS

At the time when Hardy wrote *Tess*, fairs of all kinds formed a major part of rural trade patterns. There were live-stock fairs, cheese fairs, and 'mop' fairs where the hiring of new labour took place. As in the fair that Tess comes across one Saturday, dancing and drinking were a common feature of such gatherings, and, coupled with extended licensing hours, they provided a rare opportunity for hard-worked domestic and field hands to forget their cares — if only for a while.

John Holland: All the Fun of the Fair/Fine Art Photographic Library

Constable: Stonehenge (detail): Victoria & Albert Museum/Bridgeman

Primitive scene
(left) Reunited at last with her beloved Angel, Tess makes one last desperate attempt at happiness. They flee together at night, finding their way at last to Stonehenge. "I like very much to be here," Tess murmurs. "It is so solemn and lonely – after my great happiness – with nothing but the sky above my face." Peacefully, she falls asleep, feeling that "there were no folks in the world but we two," but she is woefully wrong. They are far from alone, as Angel soon discovers, and once again Tess is made to pay for her past.

CHARACTERS IN FOCUS

Tess is Hardy's most poignant and unforgettable character. He himself would talk of her as if she had been living, and it is as though the entire novel is dedicated to her, almost as an act of devotion. We learn about the people in Tess's world as she experiences them, and although Alec and Angel appear to be complete opposites, each in his own way comes close to destroying her. Yet, through all her suffering, Tess achieves a larger-than-life stature.

WHO'S WHO

Tess Durbeyfield The beautiful but doomed heroine of the novel who represents all that Hardy most admired in women. Her purity of nature and steadfastness in her love for Angel make her almost too good for this world.

Angel Clare Soft-spoken, tender and caring, he excites undying devotion in Tess. But something unyielding in his nature is his – and Tess's – undoing.

Alec d'Urberville The personification of selfish desire and indulgence, Alec robs Tess of her maidenhood and is responsible, ultimately, for her downfall.

Retty Priddle, Marian and Izz Huett The three fresh young milkmaids at Talbothays who share a room with Tess and are all half in love with Angel Clare.

John Durbeyfield Tess's feckless father whose discovery of noble lineage goes straight to his head, filling him with greed.

Joan Durbeyfield A good woman who loves all her children but is singularly lacking in wisdom.

Dairyman Crick The warm, beneficent master dairyman at Talbothays, who is kind to Tess.

Farmer Groby The man who, resenting Tess's refined manner, makes her winter at Flintcombe-Ash especially harsh.

Mr Clare Angel's father, an honest parson who divides the world into believers and non-believers, but has a good heart.

R. Redgrave: Going to Service (detail)/Fine Art Photographic Library

Charles Edward Wilson: At the Stile: The Milkmaid. Christie's, London/Bridgeman Art Library

Angel Clare (above) was to Tess "all that goodness could be – knew all that a guide, philosopher, and friend should know" and was the "right and desired" man whom she should have met first had Fate not intervened. But, given the turn of events, Angel finds himself unable to understand or forgive her. When he eventually comes to his senses, it is too late.

Tess's workmates (below), Retty Priddle and Marian and Izz Huett lose their beloved Angel to her with good grace: "You will think of us when you be his wife, Tess, and of how we told 'ee that we loved him, and how we . . . could not hate you, because you were his choice . . ."

Basil Bradley: Feeding the Calves/Fine Art Photographic Library

Endowed with "a luxuriance of aspect, a fulness of growth, which made her appear more of a woman than she really was," Tess (above) captivates virtually everyone she meets. But her unconscious and indeed unwanted sensuality gain the attentions of Alec d'Urberville, and once beheld by him, her fate is sealed. He tries to woo her first with words, then with money and, ultimately, when she remains steadfast in her rejection of him, he forcibly takes what he wants. He declares, "You can hold your own for beauty against any woman of these parts, gentle or simple; I say it to you as a practical man and well-wisher."

To Angel Clare, Tess appears "a fresh and virginal daughter of Nature", embodying all that he wants in a woman, a lover and a wife, until he learns that his idealized virgin is not as he imagined.

"Durbeyfield (right) was what was locally called a slack-twisted fellow; he had good strength to work at times; but the times could not be relied on to coincide with the hours of requirement." His wife (below), by contrast was overworked but good-humoured, with the "intelligence . . . of a happy child". Hearing of their 'noble lineage' they hatch the fateful plan "to send Tess to claim kin", inadvertently sending her to her doom.

"I suppose I am a bad fellow – a damn bad fellow", Alec d'Urberville (left) confesses. "I was born bad, and I shall die bad in all probability". But he does not realize the harm he has done poor Tess, she being far too proud to contact him or ask for his help. Later, he reforms, proclaiming his new-found spirituality to all who will listen. "He had, he said, been the greatest of sinners. He had scoffed; he had wantonly associated with the reckless and the lewd. But a day of awakening had come . . . by the grace of Heaven . . ." Tess hears the words but is unconvinced, and rightly so. Meeting her again after a long absence he says "You haunt me. Those very eyes that you turned upon me with such a bitter flash a moment ago, they come to me just as you showed them then, in the night and in the day!" And although desperation forces her back to him, she never stops despising him for his depravity of spirit.

POETIC VISION

Although novel-writing had sustained him financially for so long, the moral outcry which his later fiction provoked made Hardy doubly intent on returning to his first love – poetry.

The smile on your mouth was the deadest thing
Alive enough to have strength to die;
And a grin of bitterness swept thereby
Like an ominous bird a-wing . . .
NEUTRAL TONES

Hardy always considered himself a poet, but it is not surprising that he is best known as a novelist, since his 17 novels include some that would appear high on many readers' lists of 'Top Ten'. Yet ironically, Hardy was never particularly interested in his fiction. He dismissed novel writing as just a 'trade' which he had been forced to take up to make ends meet. For him poetry was the highest art. He started out as a poet and ended as one, writing nothing but poetry for the last 29 years of his life.

As a teenager, Hardy read all the poets he could, from classical to contemporary. Yet his great strength was that he chose to fashion himself into a home-made poet. He never felt that he had to submit himself to any one particular form or subject matter, or that he had to use obscure, learned allusions, or that he should absorb other poets' literary man-

Black is night's cope;
But death will not appal
One who, past doubtings all,
Waits in unhope.
IN TENEBRIS I

nerisms. He knew how he wanted to write, and he never deviated. Hardy at 80 writes like Hardy in his 30s, which is what makes it so difficult to date many of his poems accurately. Throughout his long career, his poetry is characterized by his simple, direct language, his haunting rhythms, and the imaginative intensity and precision of his images.

One of his greatest poems is *Neutral Tones* (1867), believed to be about his love for the 16-year-old Tryphena Sparks. In it he seizes on a momentary event – two lovers standing by a pond – and fills it with the pain the lovers would have felt on learning that they were cousins and that their love could never be.

The smile on your mouth was the deadest thing
Alive enough to have strength to die;
And a grin of bitterness swept thereby
Like an ominous bird a-wing . . .

Exceptional though it is, the poem was not published for another 31 years because Hardy could not find a publisher for it. Unable to make money from his poetry, Hardy contemplated being an art critic or an architect, but settled instead on novel writing when his third work, *Under the Greenwood Tree* (1872), received encouraging reviews. And this is how he earned his living for the next 24 years. From the age of 27 until in his mid-50s Hardy was a reluctant but successful novelist.

Although he did not abandon poetry during this period, any poems that he did write

H.E. Bowler: The Doubt: Tate Gallery, London

L.C. Taylor: Persuasion/Fine Art Photographic Library

were 'consigned to the darkness'. And in his notebooks he never stopped yearning for 'the essence of all imaginative and emotional literature.' In 1879 he explained that 'The ultimate aim of the poet should be to touch our hearts by showing us his own', and even in 1890, before two of his greatest novels (*Tess of the d'Urbervilles* and *Jude the Obscure*) were published, his heart was with (to quote Keats) "the viewless wings of poesy".

UNWILLING OUTCAST

Intent though he was to devote himself to poetry, he did not finally do so until five years later, when he had already made his way as a novelist. It is true that Hardy's turning to poetry was partly prompted by his despair at Victorian conservatism – expressed in the moral outcry that *Tess* and *Jude* had caused. Hardy confirmed this in his pointed attack on the ways in which people read novels and poems differently. In novels, a blasphemous idea can bring down a 'sneering', 'foaming' outrage. In poetry, he argued, Galileo's radical assertion 'that the world moved' would have escaped even the eagle-eyed Inquisition. For Hardy, writing poetry was clearly going to be less controversial.

Yet the changeover was also influenced by a number of other factors. Hardy did not want to become a social outcast – criticism of his

work cut him deeply; he had begun to find writing novels extremely demanding; too many personal elements were intruding into his narratives for his comfort; and *Jude* had so alienated his wife Emma that she no longer wanted to copy out his work. This last factor was particularly important given that Hardy had bad arthritis in his hands.

Jude was Hardy's last novel. From 1896 onwards he returned to his first love, poetry. Momentary fears that he had lost his poetic touch were flung aside by the sheer volume and quality of poems which he now poured out. From 1898 to 1928, he published seven collections of verse. One more was published posthumously. In this second part of his writing career (29 years, almost as long as his time engaged in writing novels) he wrote over 900 poems. An average of nearly three a month does not make him prolific, but he was immensely consistent. Poetry was for him a necessity. He tackled any subject from the smallest, most seemingly trivial detail:

You stand so stock-still that your ear-ring shakes
At each pulsation which the vein there makes;

to despairing anti-war pronouncements:

After two thousand years of mass
We've got as far as poison gas!

But the two most striking elements of his poetry are his use of natural imagery, and themes of lost or ill-starred love.

You stand so stock-still that your
ear-ring shakes
At each pulsation which the vein
there makes.
AT WYNYARD'S GAP

Eugene de Blaas: A Beauty/Private Collection/Fine Art Photographic Library

Nature is an inevitable backdrop, metaphor and subject. In the *Darkling Thrush* (1900) (see page 89) and *Afterwards* (1917), for example, he displays his extraordinary observation of nature, fusing his sharpness of vision with his natural poetic imagery. In the first poem, when his muse had gone, leaving behind a broken lyre, its strings are cleverly pictured as *"the tangled bine-stems [that] scored the sky"*, with the once fertile earth being reduced to the image of a tough, leathery, shrunken death. And in the second poem, a landing hawk is likened to, of all things, *"an eyelid's soundless blink"*, a powerful, extraordinary image.

Hardy reconstructs Nature imaginatively, precisely and memorably. But his greatest achievements are perhaps his love lyrics. These were prompted in 1912 by the death of his first wife, Emma. Later he read her scathing notes 'What I think of my Husband', which added to his guilt for his maltreatment of her, and increased the intensity of this creative outburst. A love that had died 20 years before suddenly revived.

The first group of poems about her, entitled *Poems 1912-13*, contain many of the finest love lyrics in the language. Although the title appears starkly unemotional, it was more graphically subtitled 'moments of an ancient blaze'. *The Voice, After a Journey, Beeny Cliff, The Phantom Horsewoman* and *I Found Her Out There* touch our hearts, just as Hardy said he

Arthur Hacker: Shimmering Summer/Fine Art Photographic Library

'Where is she?' I said:
– 'Who?' they asked that sat there;
'Not a soul's come in sight.'
– 'A maid with red hair.'
– 'Ah.' They paled. 'She is dead.

People see her at night,
But you are the first
On whom she has burst
In the keen common light.'
THE GLIMPSE

> – 'I wish I had feathers, a fine sweeping gown,
> And a delicate face, and could strut about Town!' –
> 'My dear – a raw country girl, such as you be,
> Cannot quite expect that. You ain't ruined,' said she.
>
> THE RUINED MAID

Garreta: Portrait of a Young Lady/Fine Art Photographic Library

That the woman beside her was first his choice".

And *The Ruined Maid* explores the fate of a woman who is possessed not by herself but by others. Hardy does not, however, see her as 'ruined' or corrupt in any way since she has clearly benefited by the choices she has made.

One of Hardy's strengths is that he did not only write about women from his own viewpoint, but also made them his narrators, berating men for their callous behaviour. In *Lost Love* the speaker wonders "*why such a woman as I was born!*", as her ex-lover passes her door without stopping. Impermanent relationships and lost love are themes which Hardy grapples with again and again, honing them into aching verse such as the stirring:

> *Not a line of her writing have I,*
> *Not a thread of her hair.*

Hardy continued writing poetry to within a month of his death, when he was 87. His final collection, *Winter Words*, was still being prepared when the end came. His impact since then on other poets has been enormous, possibly greater than any other 20th-century poet. Robert Graves, Philip Larkin, Ezra Pound and John Betjeman have all acknowledged his rich, haunting and powerful influence. Selecting the best of Hardy's fiction is no problem; agreeing on his finest poems is quite a task. In his lifetime he wrote on every conceivable subject, although the largest group – all of which refer to his first wife Emma – is arguably the best.

was going to do. Once read, it is impossible to forget his fine, poignant lines:

> Woman much missed, how you call to me, call to me,
>   Saying that now you are not as you were

and:

>   O the opal and the sapphire of that wandering western sea,
> And the woman riding high above with bright hair flapping free –

or his 'Hardyisms', such as 'I lipped her' for I kissed her.

Grand lines alternate with painfully understated images in nearly 200 poems about Emma. The poems became charged with his complex feelings for her, as he repeatedly mined the past, putting virtually every aspect of their relationship under the microscope. He reproached himself for ignoring her in *The Going*, and recalled her love of daisies in *Rain on a Grave*, and their first meeting in *The Change*. It was a sustained, deeply-felt return to the past.

Hardy's love was always more ideal than actual, tending to flourish when confronted by separation or loss. On the written page, if not in practice, he cared about the loveless and the fallen. In *At Tea* he tackles the question of triangles – the 'other woman' sits beside "*the happy young housewife [who] does not know/*

Vilhelm Hammershøi: Interior/Fine Art Photographic Library

> *I rose and neared the window-glass,*
> *But vanished thence had she:*
> *Only a pallid moth, alas,*
> *Tapped at the pane for me.*
>
> SOMETHING TAPPED

SELECTED POEMS

After giving up writing novels, Hardy wrote more than 900 poems between 1898 and 1928. His intense emotional and symbolic response to Nature – so central to his novels – is the focus of such poems as *The Darkling Thrush*. But another major theme is love – usually lost love. And the poems written to his first wife Emma after her death in 1912 (see overleaf) are among his most poignant. Often in these poems there is a dual emotion, as remembered joy seems to heighten present sadness.

In *The Dream is – Which?*, "a curtain drops between" his youthful moments of shared happiness and his lonely old age. *The Voice* and *Beeny Cliff* are also haunting celebrations of the past, in which Hardy's sensitivity to the natural world merges with his feelings for his dead wife.

In *Something Tapped*, the poet hears a tap on the window pane, and imagines his "weary Belovéd's face" beckoning him. But he discovers it is only a "pallid moth" tapping. There is a similar sad juxtaposition of images in *Two Lips*: he kisses her first "in love, in troth, in laughter" – and "in a shroud thereafter".

Hardy is honest enough to recognize that these poems do not reflect how he treated Emma when she was alive, and in *An Upbraiding* he assumes her voice: when they are reunited in death, she asks, will he treat her as "cold/As when we lived" or as tenderly as he remembers her?

Neils H. Christiansen: Snowy Landscape/Fine Art Photographic Library

The Darkling Thrush

I leant upon a coppice gate
    When Frost was spectre-gray,
And Winter's dregs made desolate
    The weakening eye of day.
The tangled bine-stems scored the sky
    Like strings of broken lyres,
And all mankind that haunted nigh
    Had sought their household fires.

The land's sharp features seemed to be
    The Century's corpse outleant,
His crypt the cloudy canopy,
    The wind his death-lament.
The ancient pulse of germ and birth
    Was shrunken hard and dry,
And every spirit upon earth
    Seemed fervourless as I.

At once a voice arose among
    The bleak twigs overhead
In a full-hearted evensong
    Of joy illimited;
An aged thrush, frail, gaunt, and small,
    In blast-beruffled plume,
Had chosen thus to fling his soul
    Upon the growing gloom.

So little cause for carolings
    Of such ecstatic sound
Was written on terrestrial things
    Afar or nigh around,
That I could think there trembled through
    His happy good-night air
Some blessed Hope, whereof he knew
    And I was unaware.

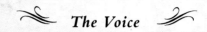

EMMA HARDY
1840—1912

The Voice

Woman much missed, how you call to me, call to me,
Saying that now you are not as you were
When you had changed from the one who was all to me,
But as at first, when our day was fair.

Can it be you that I hear? Let me view you, then,
Standing as when I drew near to the town
Where you would wait for me: yes, as I knew you then,
Even to the original air-blue gown!

Or is it only the breeze, in its listlessness
Travelling across the wet mead to me here,
You being ever dissolved to wan wistlessness,
Heard no more again far or near?

Thus I; faltering forward,
Leaves around me falling,
Wind oozing thin through the thorn from norward,
And the woman calling.

The Dream Is – Which?

I am laughing by the brook with her,
    Splashed in its tumbling stir;
And then it is a blankness looms
    As if I walked not there,
Nor she, but found me in haggard rooms,
    And treading a lonely stair.

With radiant cheeks and rapid eyes
    We sit where none espies;
Till a harsh change comes edging in
    As no such scene were there,
But winter, and I were bent and thin,
    And cinder-gray my hair.

We dance in heys around the hall,
    Weightless as thistleball;
And then a curtain drops between,
    As if I danced not there,
But wandered through a mounded green
    To find her, I knew where.

An Upbraiding

Now I am dead you sing to me
    The songs we used to know,
But while I lived you had no wish
    Or care for doing so.

Now I am dead you come to me
    In the moonlight, comfortless;
Ah, what would I have given alive
    To win such tenderness!

When you are dead, and stand to me
    Not differenced, as now,
But like again, will you be cold
    As when we lived, or how?

THOMAS HARDY
1840 — 1928

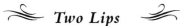 **Two Lips**

I kissed them in fancy as I came
Away in the morning glow:
I kissed them through the glass of her picture-frame:
She did not know.

I kissed them in love, in troth, in laughter,
When she knew all; long so!
That I should kiss them in a shroud thereafter
She did not know.

 Beeny Cliff

I

the opal and the sapphire of that wandering western sea,
d the woman riding high above with bright hair flapping free —
e woman whom I loved so, and who loyally loved me.

II

e pale mews plained below us, and the waves seemed far away
a nether sky, engrossed in saying their ceaseless babbling say,
we laughed light-heartedly aloft on that clear-sunned March day.

III

little cloud then cloaked us, and there flew an irised rain,
d the Atlantic dyed its levels with a dull misfeatured stain,
d then the sun burst out again, and purples prinked the main.

IV

Still in all its chasmal beauty bulks old Beeny to the sky,
d shall she and I not go there once again now March is nigh,
d the sweet things said in that March say anew there by and by?

V

at if still in chasmal beauty looms that wild weird western shore,
e woman now is – elsewhere – whom the ambling pony bore,
d nor knows nor cares for Beeny, and will laugh there nevermore.

 Something Tapped

Something tapped on the pane of my room
When there was never a trace
Of wind or rain, and I saw in the gloom
My weary Belovéd's face.

'O I am tired of waiting,' she said,
'Night, morn, noon, afternoon;
So cold it is in my lonely bed,
And I thought you would join me soon!'

I rose and neared the window-glass,
But vanished thence had she:
Only a pallid moth, alas,
Tapped at the pane for me.

Yesterday's Harvest

The Wessex farm-life which Hardy so lovingly depicted was long gone when he wrote his novels. It was a way of life both brutal and tender, bitter and, for some, sadly missed.

Oh! There's nothing in life like making love
Save making hay in fine weather.

So wrote the poet Thomas Hood (1799–1845), encapsulating the romanticized view of Nature popular in the 19th century. The image of an idyllic, pre-industrial world is a familiar one, reflected in the paintings and photographs of the era, but it is misleading. This image is partly fostered by nostalgia and partly by the limitations of Victorian photography.

At the time, photographs had to be taken in good light and the need for long exposures called for posed groups, not action shots. Thus scenes of happy harvesters standing proudly beside their haywagon or resting in fields under a hot sun are common. What the pictures do not show are exhausted labourers in wet fields.

As a man, Thomas Hardy tended towards sentimentality and nostalgia. But as a writer, he struggled for a truer, less romanticized image of country ways. Farm life represented much that he cherished, but he also recognized that it involved extremely long hours of hard work and poor pay.

Although Hardy never worked on the land himself, he had a profound knowledge of the countryside, and in the introduction to the 'Wessex Edition' of his novels

The rural idyll
(right) The modern image of lost rural bliss is familiar to everyone from paintings and old photographs such as this. Man and beast exist in harmony with a fruitful earth; reality was often very different.

BBC Hulton Picture Library

Steam-driven monster
(below) The threshing machine brought new speed and efficiency to harvesting, but the labourers who had to feed it were made to suffer by the incessant noise and heat.

Museum of English Rural Life, Reading

Dorset County Museum/MERL, Reading

(1912) he wrote 'I have instituted inquiries to correct tricks of memory, and striven against temptations to exaggerate, in order to preserve for my own satisfaction a fairly true record of a vanishing life.'

During Hardy's long lifetime, the industrialization of England steadily increased, but in the mid-19th century, farming was still the single greatest source of employment. The Commissioners for the Census of 1861 in England and Wales referred to those working on the land as 'the great central productive class of the country in which 2,010,454 people are employed'. At this time the population of England and Wales was just over 20 million and slightly less than half lived in rural areas.

In Dorset, agriculture remained the chief source of livelihood long after it had ceased to be so in most other parts of the country. Its mild climate and excellent soil make it a strongly agricultural county to-day. In Hardy's time dairy farms mushroomed in the river valleys, and the chalk downlands were the home of large flocks of sheep. The majority of farms, however, depended on both crops and livestock.

Like the land itself, the men and women who worked it varied greatly in status and prosperity. At the top end of the scale were gentlemen farmers who could afford to employ stewards or bailiffs to look after the day-to-day running of their estates, and at the bottom were peasant farmers who worked a plot of land single-handed. Some farmers were only part-timers, and Hardy portrays such a character in *The Return of the Native* – Damon Wildeve, who is a publican and also farms reclaimed heathland.

LANDOWNERS AND TENANTS

About half the agricultural land in Dorset was worked by the employees of big landowners or by smaller independent farmers; the other half was leased to tenant farmers. In the 18th century the leases had sometimes been handed on from generation to generation, but by the middle of the 19th century, they were often granted only for short terms and could change hands rapidly. Those tenants who prospered tended to move to larger farms, but those who were unable to pay the rent were likely to be evicted. In *Far From the Madding Crowd*, Bathsheba fears this will happen to her because her husband, Sergeant Troy, has been sorely neglecting the farm.

Success or failure depended on different factors, and there were cycles of prosperity and depression throughout the 19th century. At the beginning of the century, for example, the Napoleonic Wars meant that little foodstuff could be imported, so demand for homegrown produce was great and there were handsome profits to be made. A depression followed this boom period, followed by gradual recovery, thanks partly to the implementation of more scientific

Woollen wealth

(below) Sheep-shearing was a valued skill; the faster the shearer, the more he could earn. But although itinerant workers might make 'big money' in agricultural terms, the season was necessarily a short one.

Hand labour

(right) Despite increasing sophistication, farming in the mid-19th century depended largely on methods that had changed little over the centuries. The scythe was known more than 4000 years ago.

MERL, Reading

methods of draining the land and soil fertilization.

The late 1870s was marked by another depression, brought on by a series of bad harvests which coincided with the beginning of large-scale importation of corn from North America. (Frozen meat from the Americas, Australia and New Zealand followed soon afterwards.) And apart from these historical factors the farmer was always at the mercy of the weather. An exceptionally bad harvest would obviously mean there was little to sell, but an exceptionally good harvest could also hurt the farmer by making the price of produce too low.

Hardy began his writing career when farming in Dorset was going through one of its most prosperous periods. A 'typical' farm of this period (according to a report of the Royal Commission on the Employment of Children, Young Persons and Women in Agriculture of 1868) consisted of 660 acres. About 500 acres was arable, the rest divided into pasture and downland: 29 men and boys were employed throughout the year, and four more men and 11 women were taken on during the harvest. Of the permanent staff, eight cared for the horses and five for the sheep, cows and other animals; the remaining 16 were labourers and plough boys. The total wage bill for the year was £788, making the average wage around 10 shillings a week.

At this time there was little mechanization on Dorset farms, but in the last quarter of the century, it began to have an impact. Initially farmers tended not to buy the new machines (which were needed only at certain times of the year), but to hire them from external contractors. One such firm was Eddison's Steam Plough Works, founded in Dorchester in 1870. Its factory hooter, going off at 5.45 am every morning, caused great annoyance to Hardy and other local residents. The new machines were greeted with suspicion by the men whose work they replaced, especially as the engineers who handled them generally earned two or three times as much as a labourer. In *Tess of the d'Urbervilles* one such engineer is described as "in the agricultural world, but not of it".

In *The Mayor of Casterbridge* Hardy describes the impact of one of these machines – the seed drill – saying it created "*about as much sensation in the corn-market as a*

Dressing the wheel
(above) A miller gouges new grooves in his mill wheel so that it will grind more efficiently. The miller was a figure as central to any community as the vicar or squire.

A new thatch
(below) Thatching is one of the few old rural crafts to have survived the coming of mechanization, and it still conjures up the romance of the past.

flying machine would at Charing Cross". Donald Farfrae says, "*it will revolutionise sowing hereabout! No more sowers flinging their seed about broadcast, so that some falls by the wayside and some among thorns, and all that. Each grain will go straight to its intended place.*" Seed drills were introduced to Dorset around 1850, and about ten years later horse-driven mechanical reapers came into use. More sophisticated reapers that bound the corn into sheaves did not appear until the 1890s.

HARVEST TIME

By present-day standards, farming in Hardy's day was still very labour-intensive, especially at harvest time, when overtime would be paid and extra labourers employed to speed up the work. The crops grown then were slower to mature than present-day strains, and the harvest was not usually completed until late October. If weather was bad, it could continue into December. Such a bad late harvest is described in *The Mayor of Casterbridge*, when "nearly the whole town" is out working in the fields by moonlight. Machinery did not necessarily cut down the amount of gruelling physical labour, and in some instances could add to it. The steam-driven threshing machine, one of which is described in *Tess of the d'Urbervilles*, is a case in point. 'Not a woman in the county but hates the threshing machine', wrote Hardy in *The Dorsetshire Labourer*. 'The dust, the din, the sustained exertion demanded to keep up with the steam tyrant are distasteful to all women but the coarsest.'

Whatever discomfort these workers had to endure, they at least had the company of their fellow labourers. The life of the shepherd was by contrast lonely as well as hard. This was particularly so in the lambing season, and in *Far From the Madding Crowd* Hardy vividly describes Gabriel Oak's "enforced nightly attendance" on his flock. He sleeps near the sheep in a small hut on just "a few corn sacks". Sheep not only supplied

BBC Hulton Picture Library

Money in milk
(left and below) Dairy
farming had a buoyant,
expanding market in
Hardy's time. As well as
milk, butter, cream and
cheese, it provided – in the
waste products of skimmed
milk – food that could
support the farmyard pigs.
Dairy farmers also enjoyed
the benefit of not being as
vulnerable to bad harvests or
gluts as arable farmers were,
and so could maintain a
flourishing business.

Man and machine
(bottom) Farm machinery
brought out the Victorian
genius for mechanical
invention. The 'Fowler
Steam Ploughing Tackle'
featured a pair of rigs (only
one is seen here) drawn by
stout cables to the steam
engine. Mechanization
came gradually, but it
eventually greatly reduced
the size of the workforce
required on farms,
increasing the drift of
labourers to the towns.

meat and wool, but also were used to fertilize arable land. At night they would be moved from their grazing land to the arable fields, and the position of their pens was changed from night to night so that the whole field was manured.

The life of the shepherd had changed little over the centuries and followed a regular seasonal rhythm. Lambing took place in late winter or early spring, and shearing around May or June. Often the shearing was done with the help of travelling specialists. They used hand-shears and it was time-consuming work – Gabriel Oak's time of 23½ minutes to shear a sheep was the quickest Bathsheba had ever witnessed. In autumn some of the flock would usually be sold at market.

While sheep farming represented unbroken links with the past, dairy farming reflected changes in the social scene. In the second half of the 19th century there was a great increase in the demand for milk in the rapidly expanding towns. Quick rail transport (the railway came to Dorchester in 1847) made it possible to send milk into the cities. Hardy's heroine Tess works for Dairyman Crick, who sends his milk to London in this way. As Tess takes the churns to the station she is amused to think of the various different people who will drink it: "*Noble men and noble women, ambassadors and centurions, ladies and tradeswomen, and babies who have never seen a cow.*" Pasteurization and sterilization were not introduced until about 1910, so in hot weather the milk sometimes went sour en route.

In spite of mechanization, all milking was still done by hand – it was only after World War I that milking machinery became common. Most of the milking was done by women in two sessions, at 3–4am and in the afternoon. Milking out of doors in good weather could be a very pleasant job, but the flies that massed in dirty cowsheds and made the animals restless could turn the work into a nightmare. Standards of hygiene varied greatly from farm to farm, and Dairyman Crick

BBC Hulton Picture Library

BBC Hulton Picture Library

Plenty and poverty
For those who could capitalize on the fertile potential of the Wessex countryside (such as the owners and dealers, right) Hardy's was a boom time. For labourers (below), faced with little security of tenure, more mechanization, periodic slumps and callous exploitation, there was often anxiety, disease and a risk of starvation in a land of plenty.

rebukes a milker who has not washed her hands properly, saying "*Upon my soul, if the London folk only knowed of thee and thy slovenly ways, they'd swaller their milk and butter more mincing than they do a'ready.*"

Hardy's novels touch on most aspects of contemporary agricultural life, and he also wrote an important non-fiction work embracing the subject – *The Dorsetshire Labourer*, published in *Longman's Magazine* in July 1883. In this Hardy says that the unpleasantness of the farm labourer's life stemmed not so much from the hardness and monotony of the work as 'from a sense of incertitude and precariousness of their position'. They had to seek work at annual hiring fairs and whereas a generation earlier there had been some sense of stability, they 'now look upon an annual removal as the most natural thing in the world'.

Hardy thought that 'drudgery in the fields resulted at worst in a mood of painless passivity'. But by present-day standards their living conditions seem appalling. Their homes were generally overcrowded, sometimes to an almost unbelievable degree. One cottage mentioned in the 1861 Census housed 35 people, and the 1868 Royal Commission mentions a family of eight living in an outhouse intended for a calf. Sanitation was primitive, with water having to be carried from the nearest pump, stream or well. There was no means of heating it except over an open fire, so trying to maintain decent standards of cleanliness must have been gruelling work, especially when there were several children in the family (for couples who married in 1860 seven children was the national average). Hardy's Tess comes upon her mother "*amid the group of children . . . hanging over the Monday washing-tub, which had now, as always, lingered on to the end of the week*".

By the time of Hardy's death – indeed by the time he finished his career as a novelist in the 1890s – the type of country life he described in his books was disappearing. By the turn of the century three people lived in the town for every one that lived in the country. Hardy must have regretted the passing of a way of rural life that was the fountainhead of his creativity, and that his books immortalized.

BIBLIOGRAPHY

Baker, George P., *Charles Dickens and Maria Beadnell* (reprint of 1908 edition). Folcroft (Folcroft, 1974)

Bernier, Olivier, *The Secrets of Marie Antoinette*. Doubleday (New York, 1985)

Besan, Walter, *London in the Nineteenth Century*. Garland Publishing (New York, 1985)

Birch, Una, *Secret Societies and the French Revolution*. Gordon Press (New York, 1976)

Boumelha, Penny, *Thomas Hardy and Women: Sexual Ideology and Narrative Form*. University of Wisconsin Press (Madison, 1982)

Bowra, C. M., *The Lyrical Poetry of Thomas Hardy*. Haskell (Brooklyn, 1975)

Brady, Kristin, *The Short Stories of Thomas Hardy*. St Martin's Press (New York, 1982)

Brennecke, E., *The Life of Thomas Hardy* (reprint of 1925 edition). Haskell (Brooklyn, 1973)

Browne, Edgar, *Phiz and Dickens* (reprint of 1914 edition). Haskell (Brooklyn, 1972)

Burton, Richard, *Charles Dickens: How to Know Him*. Folcroft (Folcroft, 1919)

Butler, L. J., *Thomas Hardy*. Cambridge University Press (New York, 1978)

Charpentier, John, *Rousseau: The Child of Nature* (reprint of 1931 edition). Richard West (Philadelphia, 1973)

Clemens, Cyril, *My Chat with Thomas Hardy*. Folcroft (Folcroft, 1944)

Cobban, Alfred B., *Social Interpretation of the French Revolution*. Cambridge University Press (New York, 1968)

Crosby, Travis L., *Sir Robert Peel's Administration*. Shoe String Press (Hamden, 1976)

Davie, Donald, *Thomas Hardy and British Poetry*. Oxford Univiersity Press (New York, 1972)

Dello Buono, Carmen J., *Rare Early Essays on Charles Dickens*. Norwood Editions (Norwood, 1980)

Dickinson, H. T., *British Radicalism and the French Revolution, 1789-1815*. Basil Blackwell (New York, 1985)

Doyle, William, *Origins of the French Revolution*. Oxford University Press (New York, 1980)

Fields, James T., *In and Out of Doors with Charles Dickens* (reprint of 1876 edition). AMS Press (New York, 1976)

Fitzgerald, Percy, *Life of Charles Dickens,* 2 vols. (reprint of 1905 edition). Richard West (Philadelphia, 1973)

Giordano, Frank R., Jr., *I'd Have My Life Unbe: Thomas Hardy's Self-Destructive Characters*. University of Alabama Press (Tuscaloosa, 1984)

Gissing, George, *Charles Dickens*. Haskell (Brooklyn, 1974)

Gooch, George P., *Louis the Fifteenth: The Monarchy in Decline* (reprint of 1956 edition). Greenwood Press (Westport, 1976)

Hardy, Barbara, *The Moral Art of Dickens*. Humanities Press International (Atlantic Highlands, 1985)

Jackson, Thomas, *Charles Dickens: Progress of a Radical* (reprint of 1937 edition). Haskell (Brooklyn, 1971)

Jones, E. L., *Development of English Agriculture, 1815-1873*. Humanities Press International (Atlantic Highlands, 1968)

Kaplan, Fred, *Dickens and Mesmerism: The Hidden Springs of Fiction*. Princeton University Press (Princeton, 1975)

Mason, Haydn, *Voltaire: A Biography*. Johns Hopkins University Press (Baltimore, 1981)

Mason, John H., *The Irresistible Diderot*. Salem House (Topsfield, 1984)

Miller, J. Hillis, *Thomas Hardy: Distance and Desire*. Harvard University Press (Cambridge, 1970)

Miltoun, Francis, *Dickens' London* (reprint of 1904 edition). Richard West (Philadelphia, 1973)

Priestley, J. B., *Charles Dickens and His World*. Scribner (New York, 1978)

Redcliffe Press Ltd, ed., *Dorset Essays*. State Mutual Book (New York, 1983)

Rutland, William R., *Thomas Hardy: A Study of His Writings and Their Background* (reprint of 1938 edition). Russell & Russell (New York, 1962)

Shore, W. Teignmouth, *Charles Dickens and His Friends* (reprint of 1909 edition). Richard West (Philadelphia, 1973)

Sime, J. G., *Thomas Hardy of the Wessex Novels*. Folcroft (Folcroft, 1928)

Weber, Carl, *Thomas Hardy in Maine*. Haskell (Brooklyn, 1975)

INDEX